ISBN 0-8373-0060-6

C-60    CAREER EXAMINATION SERIES

*This is your*
*PASSBOOK® for...*

# Auditor

*Test Preparation Study Guide*

*Questions & Answers*

**NATIONAL LEARNING CORPORATION**

Copyright © 2010 by

# National Learning Corporation

### 212 Michael Drive, Syosset, New York 11791

(516) 921-8888
(800) 645-6337
FAX: (516) 921-8743
www.passbooks.com
sales @ passbooks.com
info @ passbooks.com

PRINTED IN THE UNITED STATES OF AMERICA

# PASSBOOK®
## NOTICE

# PASSBOOK SERIES®

THE *PASSBOOK SERIES®* has been created to prepare applicants and candidates for the ultimate academic battlefield – the examination room.

At some time in our lives, each and every one of us may be required to take an examination – for validation, matriculation, admission, qualification, registration, certification, or licensure.

Based on the assumption that every applicant or candidate has met the basic formal educational standards, has taken the required number of courses, and read the necessary texts, the *PASSBOOK SERIES®* furnishes the one special preparation which may assure passing with confidence, instead of failing with insecurity. Examination questions – together with answers – are furnished as the basic vehicle for study so that the mysteries of the examination and its compounding difficulties may be eliminated or diminished by a sure method.

This book is meant to help you pass your examination provided that you qualify and are serious in your objective.

The entire field is reviewed through the huge store of content information which is succinctly presented through a provocative and challenging approach – the question-and-answer method.

A climate of success is established by furnishing the correct answers at the end of each test.

You soon learn to recognize types of questions, forms of questions, and patterns of questioning. You may even begin to anticipate expected outcomes.

You perceive that many questions are repeated or adapted so that you can gain acute insights, which may enable you to score many sure points.

You learn how to confront new questions, or types of questions, and to attack them confidently and work out the correct answers.

You note objectives and emphases, and recognize pitfalls and dangers, so that you may make positive educational adjustments.

Moreover, you are kept fully informed in relation to new concepts, methods, practices, and directions in the field.

You discover that you are actually taking the examination all the time: you are preparing for the examination by "taking" an examination, not by reading extraneous and/or supererogatory textbooks.

In short, this PASSBOOK®, used directedly, should be an important factor in helping you to pass your test.

# AUDITOR

## DUTIES
Performs professional accounting work in making office and field audits of financial and accounting records. Verifies receipts and disbursements in accordance with prescribed audit procedures and examines for compliance with laws and regulations. Performs field audits of departmental financial and accounting records to insure compliance with legal provisions, uniform system of accounts and accepted financial administration. Observes and evaluates effectiveness of internal accounting procedures and controls. Prepares audit reports and makes recommendations for changes and improvements in accordance with findings. Does related work as required.

## SCOPE OF THE EXAMINATION
The multiple-choice written test will cover knowledge, skills, and/or abilities in such areas as:
1.  General accounting;
2.  General auditing;
3.  Governmental accounting;
4.  Preparing written material; and
5.  Understanding and interpreting tabular material.

———

# HOW TO TAKE A TEST

## I.  YOU MUST PASS AN EXAMINATION

### A.  WHAT EVERY CANDIDATE SHOULD KNOW

Examination applicants often ask us for help in preparing for the written test. What can I study in advance? What kinds of questions will be asked? How will the test be given? How will the papers be graded?

As an applicant for a civil service examination, you may be wondering about some of these things. Our purpose here is to suggest effective methods of advance study and to describe civil service examinations.

Your chances for success on this examination can be increased if you know how to prepare. Those "pre-examination jitters" can be reduced if you know what to expect. You can even experience an adventure in good citizenship if you know why civil service exams are given.

### B.  WHY ARE CIVIL SERVICE EXAMINATIONS GIVEN?

Civil service examinations are important to you in two ways. As a citizen, you want public jobs filled by employees who know how to do their work. As a job seeker, you want a fair chance to compete for that job on an equal footing with other candidates. The best-known means of accomplishing this two-fold goal is the competitive examination.

Exams are widely publicized throughout the nation. They may be administered for jobs in federal, state, city, municipal, town or village governments or agencies.

Any citizen may apply, with some limitations, such as the age or residence of applicants. Your experience and education may be reviewed to see whether you meet the requirements for the particular examination. When these requirements exist, they are reasonable and applied consistently to all applicants. Thus, a competitive examination may cause you some uneasiness now, but it is your privilege and safeguard.

### C.  HOW ARE CIVIL SERVICE EXAMS DEVELOPED?

Examinations are carefully written by trained technicians who are specialists in the field known as "psychological measurement," in consultation with recognized authorities in the field of work that the test will cover. These experts recommend the subject matter areas or skills to be tested; only those knowledges or skills important to your success on the job are included. The most reliable books and source materials available are used as references. Together, the experts and technicians judge the difficulty level of the questions.

Test technicians know how to phrase questions so that the problem is clearly stated. Their ethics do not permit "trick" or "catch" questions. Questions may have been tried out on sample groups, or subjected to statistical analysis, to determine their usefulness.

Written tests are often used in combination with performance tests, ratings of training and experience, and oral interviews. All of these measures combine to form the best-known means of finding the right person for the right job.

## II. HOW TO PASS THE WRITTEN TEST

### A. NATURE OF THE EXAMINATION

To prepare intelligently for civil service examinations, you should know how they differ from school examinations you have taken. In school you were assigned certain definite pages to read or subjects to cover. The examination questions were quite detailed and usually emphasized memory. Civil service exams, on the other hand, try to discover your present ability to perform the duties of a position, plus your potentiality to learn these duties. In other words, a civil service exam attempts to predict how successful you will be. Questions cover such a broad area that they cannot be as minute and detailed as school exam questions.

In the public service similar kinds of work, or positions, are grouped together in one "class." This process is known as *position-classification*. All the positions in a class are paid according to the salary range for that class. One class title covers all of these positions, and they are all tested by the same examination.

### B. FOUR BASIC STEPS

#### 1) Study the announcement

How, then, can you know what subjects to study? Our best answer is: "Learn as much as possible about the class of positions for which you've applied." The exam will test the knowledge, skills and abilities needed to do the work.

Your most valuable source of information about the position you want is the official exam announcement. This announcement lists the training and experience qualifications. Check these standards and apply only if you come reasonably close to meeting them.

The brief description of the position in the examination announcement offers some clues to the subjects which will be tested. Think about the job itself. Review the duties in your mind. Can you perform them, or are there some in which you are rusty? Fill in the blank spots in your preparation.

Many jurisdictions preview the written test in the exam announcement by including a section called "Knowledge and Abilities Required," "Scope of the Examination," or some similar heading. Here you will find out specifically what fields will be tested.

#### 2) Review your own background

Once you learn in general what the position is all about, and what you need to know to do the work, ask yourself which subjects you already know fairly well and which need improvement. You may wonder whether to concentrate on improving your strong areas or on building some background in your fields of weakness. When the announcement has specified "some knowledge" or "considerable knowledge," or has used adjectives like "beginning principles of…" or "advanced … methods," you can get a clue as to the number and difficulty of questions to be asked in any given field. More questions, and hence broader coverage, would be included for those subjects which are more important in the work. Now weigh your strengths and weaknesses against the job requirements and prepare accordingly.

#### 3) Determine the level of the position

Another way to tell how intensively you should prepare is to understand the level of the job for which you are applying. Is it the entering level? In other words, is this the position in which beginners in a field of work are hired? Or is it an intermediate or advanced level? Sometimes this is indicated by such words as "Junior" or "Senior" in the class title. Other jurisdictions use Roman numerals to designate the level – Clerk I, Clerk II, for example. The word "Supervisor" sometimes appears in the title. If the level is not indicated by the title, check the description of duties. Will you be working under very close supervision, or will you have responsibility for independent decisions in this work?

## 4) Choose appropriate study materials

Now that you know the subjects to be examined and the relative amount of each subject to be covered, you can choose suitable study materials. For beginning level jobs, or even advanced ones, if you have a pronounced weakness in some aspect of your training, read a modern, standard textbook in that field. Be sure it is up to date and has general coverage. Such books are normally available at your library, and the librarian will be glad to help you locate one. For entry-level positions, questions of appropriate difficulty are chosen – neither highly advanced questions, nor those too simple. Such questions require careful thought but not advanced training.

If the position for which you are applying is technical or advanced, you will read more advanced, specialized material. If you are already familiar with the basic principles of your field, elementary textbooks would waste your time. Concentrate on advanced textbooks and technical periodicals. Think through the concepts and review difficult problems in your field.

These are all general sources. You can get more ideas on your own initiative, following these leads. For example, training manuals and publications of the government agency which employs workers in your field can be useful, particularly for technical and professional positions. A letter or visit to the government department involved may result in more specific study suggestions, and certainly will provide you with a more definite idea of the exact nature of the position you are seeking.

## III. KINDS OF TESTS

Tests are used for purposes other than measuring knowledge and ability to perform specified duties. For some positions, it is equally important to test ability to make adjustments to new situations or to profit from training. In others, basic mental abilities not dependent on information are essential. Questions which test these things may not appear as pertinent to the duties of the position as those which test for knowledge and information. Yet they are often highly important parts of a fair examination. For very general questions, it is almost impossible to help you direct your study efforts. What we can do is to point out some of the more common of these general abilities needed in public service positions and describe some typical questions.

## 1) General information

Broad, general information has been found useful for predicting job success in some kinds of work. This is tested in a variety of ways, from vocabulary lists to questions about current events. Basic background in some field of work, such as sociology or economics, may be sampled in a group of questions. Often these are principles which have become familiar to most persons through exposure rather than through formal training. It is difficult to advise you how to study for these questions; being alert to the world around you is our best suggestion.

## 2) Verbal ability

An example of an ability needed in many positions is verbal or language ability. Verbal ability is, in brief, the ability to use and understand words. Vocabulary and grammar tests are typical measures of this ability. Reading comprehension or paragraph interpretation questions are common in many kinds of civil service tests. You are given a paragraph of written material and asked to find its central meaning.

## 3) Numerical ability

Number skills can be tested by the familiar arithmetic problem, by checking paired lists of numbers to see which are alike and which are different, or by interpreting charts and graphs. In the latter test, a graph may be printed in the test booklet which you are asked to use as the basis for answering questions.

## 4) Observation

A popular test for law-enforcement positions is the observation test. A picture is shown to you for several minutes, then taken away. Questions about the picture test your ability to observe both details and larger elements.

## 5) Following directions

In many positions in the public service, the employee must be able to carry out written instructions dependably and accurately. You may be given a chart with several columns, each column listing a variety of information. The questions require you to carry out directions involving the information given in the chart.

## 6) Skills and aptitudes

Performance tests effectively measure some manual skills and aptitudes. When the skill is one in which you are trained, such as typing or shorthand, you can practice. These tests are often very much like those given in business school or high school courses. For many of the other skills and aptitudes, however, no short-time preparation can be made. Skills and abilities natural to you or that you have developed throughout your lifetime are being tested.

Many of the general questions just described provide all the data needed to answer the questions and ask you to use your reasoning ability to find the answers. Your best preparation for these tests, as well as for tests of facts and ideas, is to be at your physical and mental best. You, no doubt, have your own methods of getting into an exam-taking mood and keeping "in shape." The next section lists some ideas on this subject.


## IV.  KINDS OF QUESTIONS

Only rarely is the "essay" question, which you answer in narrative form, used in civil service tests. Civil service tests are usually of the short-answer type. Full instructions for answering these questions will be given to you at the examination. But in case this is your first experience with short-answer questions and separate answer sheets, here is what you need to know:

## 1) Multiple-choice Questions

Most popular of the short-answer questions is the "multiple choice" or "best answer" question. It can be used, for example, to test for factual knowledge, ability to solve problems or judgment in meeting situations found at work.

A multiple-choice question is normally one of three types—

- It can begin with an incomplete statement followed by several possible endings. You are to find the one ending which *best* completes the statement, although some of the others may not be entirely wrong.
- It can also be a complete statement in the form of a question which is answered by choosing one of the statements listed.
- It can be in the form of a problem – again you select the best answer.

Here is an example of a multiple-choice question with a discussion which should give you some clues as to the method for choosing the right answer:

When an employee has a complaint about his assignment, the action which will *best* help him overcome his difficulty is to
   A. discuss his difficulty with his coworkers
   B. take the problem to the head of the organization
   C. take the problem to the person who gave him the assignment
   D. say nothing to anyone about his complaint

In answering this question, you should study each of the choices to find which is best. Consider choice "A" – Certainly an employee may discuss his complaint with fellow employees, but no change or improvement can result, and the complaint remains unresolved. Choice "B" is a poor choice since the head of the organization probably does not know what assignment you have been given, and taking your problem to him is known as "going over the head" of the supervisor. The supervisor, or person who made the assignment, is the person who can clarify it or correct any injustice. Choice "C" is, therefore, correct. To say nothing, as in choice "D," is unwise. Supervisors have and interest in knowing the problems employees are facing, and the employee is seeking a solution to his problem.

## 2) True/False Questions

The "true/false" or "right/wrong" form of question is sometimes used. Here a complete statement is given. Your job is to decide whether the statement is right or wrong.

SAMPLE: A person-to-person long-distance telephone call costs less than a station-to-station call to the same city.

This statement is wrong, or false, since person-to-person calls are more expensive.

This is not a complete list of all possible question forms, although most of the others are variations of these common types. You will always get complete directions for answering questions. Be sure you understand *how* to mark your answers – ask questions until you do.

## V. RECORDING YOUR ANSWERS

For an examination with very few applicants, you may be told to record your answers in the test booklet itself. Separate answer sheets are much more common. If this separate answer sheet is to be scored by machine – and this is often the case – it is highly important that you mark your answers correctly in order to get credit.

An electric scoring machine is often used in civil service offices because of the speed with which papers can be scored. Machine-scored answer sheets must be marked with a pencil, which will be given to you. This pencil has a high graphite content which responds to the electric scoring machine. As a matter of fact, stray dots may register as answers, so do not let your pencil rest on the answer sheet while you are pondering the correct answer. Also, if your pencil lead breaks or is otherwise defective, ask for another.

Since the answer sheet will be dropped in a slot in the scoring machine, be careful not to bend the corners or get the paper crumpled.

The answer sheet normally has five vertical columns of numbers, with 30 numbers to a column. These numbers correspond to the question numbers in your test booklet. After each number, going across the page are four or five pairs of dotted lines. These short dotted lines have small letters or numbers above them. The first two pairs may also have a "T" or "F" above the letters. This indicates that the first two pairs only are to be used if the questions are of the true-false type. If the questions are multiple choice, disregard the "T" and "F" and pay attention only to the small letters or numbers.

Answer your questions in the manner of the sample that follows:

32. The largest city in the United States is
    A. Washington, D.C.
    B. New York City
    C. Chicago
    D. Detroit
    E. San Francisco

1) Choose the answer you think is best. (New York City is the largest, so "B" is correct.)
2) Find the row of dotted lines numbered the same as the question you are answering. (Find row number 32)
3) Find the pair of dotted lines corresponding to the answer. (Find the pair of lines under the mark "B.")
4) Make a solid black mark between the dotted lines.

## VI. BEFORE THE TEST

Common sense will help you find procedures to follow to get ready for an examination. Too many of us, however, overlook these sensible measures. Indeed, nervousness and fatigue have been found to be the most serious reasons why applicants fail to do their best on civil service tests. Here is a list of reminders:

- Begin your preparation early – Don't wait until the last minute to go scurrying around for books and materials or to find out what the position is all about.
- Prepare continuously – An hour a night for a week is better than an all-night cram session. This has been definitely established. What is more, a night a

week for a month will return better dividends than crowding your study into a shorter period of time.

- Locate the place of the exam – You have been sent a notice telling you when and where to report for the examination. If the location is in a different town or otherwise unfamiliar to you, it would be well to inquire the best route and learn something about the building.

- Relax the night before the test – Allow your mind to rest. Do not study at all that night. Plan some mild recreation or diversion; then go to bed early and get a good night's sleep.

- Get up early enough to make a leisurely trip to the place for the test – This way unforeseen events, traffic snarls, unfamiliar buildings, etc. will not upset you.

- Dress comfortably – A written test is not a fashion show. You will be known by number and not by name, so wear something comfortable.

- Leave excess paraphernalia at home – Shopping bags and odd bundles will get in your way. You need bring only the items mentioned in the official notice you received; usually everything you need is provided. Do not bring reference books to the exam. They will only confuse those last minutes and be taken away from you when in the test room.

- Arrive somewhat ahead of time – If because of transportation schedules you must get there very early, bring a newspaper or magazine to take your mind off yourself while waiting.

- Locate the examination room – When you have found the proper room, you will be directed to the seat or part of the room where you will sit. Sometimes you are given a sheet of instructions to read while you are waiting. Do not fill out any forms until you are told to do so; just read them and be prepared.

- Relax and prepare to listen to the instructions

- If you have any physical problem that may keep you from doing your best, be sure to tell the test administrator. If you are sick or in poor health, you really cannot do your best on the exam. You can come back and take the test some other time.


## VII. AT THE TEST

The day of the test is here and you have the test booklet in your hand. The temptation to get going is very strong. Caution! There is more to success than knowing the right answers. You must know how to identify your papers and understand variations in the type of short-answer question used in this particular examination. Follow these suggestions for maximum results from your efforts:

### 1) Cooperate with the monitor
The test administrator has a duty to create a situation in which you can be as much at ease as possible. He will give instructions, tell you when to begin, check to see that you are marking your answer sheet correctly, and so on. He is not there to guard you, although he will see that your competitors do not take unfair advantage. He wants to help you do your best.

### 2) Listen to all instructions
Don't jump the gun! Wait until you understand all directions. In most civil service tests you get more time than you need to answer the questions. So don't be in a hurry.

Read each word of instructions until you clearly understand the meaning. Study the examples, listen to all announcements and follow directions. Ask questions if you do not understand what to do.

### 3) Identify your papers
Civil service exams are usually identified by number only. You will be assigned a number; you must not put your name on your test papers. Be sure to copy your number correctly. Since more than one exam may be given, copy your exact examination title.

### 4) Plan your time
Unless you are told that a test is a "speed" or "rate of work" test, speed itself is usually not important. Time enough to answer all the questions will be provided, but this does not mean that you have all day. An overall time limit has been set. Divide the total time (in minutes) by the number of questions to determine the approximate time you have for each question.

### 5) Do not linger over difficult questions
If you come across a difficult question, mark it with a paper clip (useful to have along) and come back to it when you have been through the booklet. One caution if you do this – be sure to skip a number on your answer sheet as well. Check often to be sure that you have not lost your place and that you are marking in the row numbered the same as the question you are answering.

### 6) Read the questions
Be sure you know what the question asks! Many capable people are unsuccessful because they failed to *read* the questions correctly.

### 7) Answer all questions
Unless you have been instructed that a penalty will be deducted for incorrect answers, it is better to guess than to omit a question.

### 8) Speed tests
It is often better NOT to guess on speed tests. It has been found that on timed tests people are tempted to spend the last few seconds before time is called in marking answers at random – without even reading them – in the hope of picking up a few extra points. To discourage this practice, the instructions may warn you that your score will be "corrected" for guessing. That is, a penalty will be applied. The incorrect answers will be deducted from the correct ones, or some other penalty formula will be used.

### 9) Review your answers
If you finish before time is called, go back to the questions you guessed or omitted to give them further thought. Review other answers if you have time.

### 10) Return your test materials
If you are ready to leave before others have finished or time is called, take ALL your materials to the monitor and leave quietly. Never take any test material with you. The monitor can discover whose papers are not complete, and taking a test booklet may be grounds for disqualification.

## VIII. EXAMINATION TECHNIQUES

1) Read the general instructions carefully. These are usually printed on the first page of the exam booklet. As a rule, these instructions refer to the timing of the examination; the fact that you should not start work until the signal and must stop work at a signal, etc. If there are any *special* instructions, such as a choice of questions to be answered, make sure that you note this instruction carefully.

2) When you are ready to start work on the examination, that is as soon as the signal has been given, read the instructions to each question booklet, underline any key words or phrases, such as *least, best, outline, describe* and the like. In this way you will tend to answer as requested rather than discover on reviewing your paper that you *listed without describing*, that you selected the *worst* choice rather than the *best* choice, etc.

3) If the examination is of the objective or multiple-choice type – that is, each question will also give a series of possible answers: A, B, C or D, and you are called upon to select the best answer and write the letter next to that answer on your answer paper – it is advisable to start answering each question in turn. There may be anywhere from 50 to 100 such questions in the three or four hours allotted and you can see how much time would be taken if you read through all the questions before beginning to answer any. Furthermore, if you come across a question or group of questions which you know would be difficult to answer, it would undoubtedly affect your handling of all the other questions.

4) If the examination is of the essay type and contains but a few questions, it is a moot point as to whether you should read all the questions before starting to answer any one. Of course, if you are given a choice – say five out of seven and the like – then it is essential to read all the questions so you can eliminate the two that are most difficult. If, however, you are asked to answer all the questions, there may be danger in trying to answer the easiest one first because you may find that you will spend too much time on it. The best technique is to answer the first question, then proceed to the second, etc.

5) Time your answers. Before the exam begins, write down the time it started, then add the time allowed for the examination and write down the time it must be completed, then divide the time available somewhat as follows:
   - If 3-1/2 hours are allowed, that would be 210 minutes. If you have 80 objective-type questions, that would be an average of 2-1/2 minutes per question. Allow yourself no more than 2 minutes per question, or a total of 160 minutes, which will permit about 50 minutes to review.
   - If for the time allotment of 210 minutes there are 7 essay questions to answer, that would average about 30 minutes a question. Give yourself only 25 minutes per question so that you have about 35 minutes to review.

6) The most important instruction is to *read each question* and make sure you know what is wanted. The second most important instruction is to *time yourself properly* so that you answer every question. The third most

important instruction is to *answer every question*. Guess if you have to but include something for each question. Remember that you will receive no credit for a blank and will probably receive some credit if you write something in answer to an essay question. If you guess a letter – say "B" for a multiple-choice question – you may have guessed right. If you leave a blank as an answer to a multiple-choice question, the examiners may respect your feelings but it will not add a point to your score. Some exams may penalize you for wrong answers, so in such cases *only*, you may not want to guess unless you have some basis for your answer.

7) Suggestions
   a. Objective-type questions
      1. Examine the question booklet for proper sequence of pages and questions
      2. Read all instructions carefully
      3. Skip any question which seems too difficult; return to it after all other questions have been answered
      4. Apportion your time properly; do not spend too much time on any single question or group of questions
      5. Note and underline key words – *all, most, fewest, least, best, worst, same, opposite,* etc.
      6. Pay particular attention to negatives
      7. Note unusual option, e.g., unduly long, short, complex, different or similar in content to the body of the question
      8. Observe the use of "hedging" words – *probably, may, most likely,* etc.
      9. Make sure that your answer is put next to the same number as the question
      10. Do not second-guess unless you have good reason to believe the second answer is definitely more correct
      11. Cross out original answer if you decide another answer is more accurate; do not erase until you are ready to hand your paper in
      12. Answer all questions; guess unless instructed otherwise
      13. Leave time for review

   b. Essay questions
      1. Read each question carefully
      2. Determine exactly what is wanted. Underline key words or phrases.
      3. Decide on outline or paragraph answer
      4. Include many different points and elements unless asked to develop any one or two points or elements
      5. Show impartiality by giving pros and cons unless directed to select one side only
      6. Make and write down any assumptions you find necessary to answer the questions
      7. Watch your English, grammar, punctuation and choice of words
      8. Time your answers; don't crowd material

8) Answering the essay question

Most essay questions can be answered by framing the specific response around several key words or ideas. Here are a few such key words or ideas:

M's: manpower, materials, methods, money, management
P's: purpose, program, policy, plan, procedure, practice, problems, pitfalls, personnel, public relations

    a. Six basic steps in handling problems:
1. Preliminary plan and background development
2. Collect information, data and facts
3. Analyze and interpret information, data and facts
4. Analyze and develop solutions as well as make recommendations
5. Prepare report and sell recommendations
6. Install recommendations and follow up effectiveness

    b. Pitfalls to avoid
1. *Taking things for granted* – A statement of the situation does not necessarily imply that each of the elements is necessarily true; for example, a complaint may be invalid and biased so that all that can be taken for granted is that a complaint has been registered
2. *Considering only one side of a situation* – Wherever possible, indicate several alternatives and then point out the reasons you selected the best one
3. *Failing to indicate follow up* – Whenever your answer indicates action on your part, make certain that you will take proper follow-up action to see how successful your recommendations, procedures or actions turn out to be
4. *Taking too long in answering any single question* – Remember to time your answers properly

## IX. AFTER THE TEST

Scoring procedures differ in detail among civil service jurisdictions although the general principles are the same. Whether the papers are hand-scored or graded by machine we have described, they are nearly always graded by number. That is, the person who marks the paper knows only the number – never the name – of the applicant. Not until all the papers have been graded will they be matched with names. If other tests, such as training and experience or oral interview ratings have been given, scores will be combined. Different parts of the examination usually have different weights. For example, the written test might count 60 percent of the final grade, and a rating of training and experience 40 percent. In many jurisdictions, veterans will have a certain number of points added to their grades.

After the final grade has been determined, the names are placed in grade order and an eligible list is established. There are various methods for resolving ties between those who get the same final grade – probably the most common is to place first the name of the person whose application was received first. Job offers are made from the eligible list in the order the names appear on it. You will be notified of your grade and your rank as soon as all these computations have been made. This will be done as rapidly as possible.

People who are found to meet the requirements in the announcement are called "eligibles." Their names are put on a list of eligible candidates. An eligible's chances of getting a job depend on how high he stands on this list and how fast agencies are filling jobs from the list.

When a job is to be filled from a list of eligibles, the agency asks for the names of people on the list of eligibles for that job. When the civil service commission receives this request, it sends to the agency the names of the three people highest on this list. Or, if the job to be filled has specialized requirements, the office sends the agency the names of the top three persons who meet these requirements from the general list.

The appointing officer makes a choice from among the three people whose names were sent to him. If the selected person accepts the appointment, the names of the others are put back on the list to be considered for future openings.

That is the rule in hiring from all kinds of eligible lists, whether they are for typist, carpenter, chemist, or something else. For every vacancy, the appointing officer has his choice of any one of the top three eligibles on the list. This explains why the person whose name is on top of the list sometimes does not get an appointment when some of the persons lower on the list do. If the appointing officer chooses the second or third eligible, the No. 1 eligible does not get a job at once, but stays on the list until he is appointed or the list is terminated.

## X. HOW TO PASS THE INTERVIEW TEST

The examination for which you applied requires an oral interview test. You have already taken the written test and you are now being called for the interview test – the final part of the formal examination.

You may think that it is not possible to prepare for an interview test and that there are no procedures to follow during an interview. Our purpose is to point out some things you can do in advance that will help you and some good rules to follow and pitfalls to avoid while you are being interviewed.

### What is an interview supposed to test?

The written examination is designed to test the technical knowledge and competence of the candidate; the oral is designed to evaluate intangible qualities, not readily measured otherwise, and to establish a list showing the relative fitness of each candidate – as measured against his competitors – for the position sought. Scoring is not on the basis of "right" and "wrong," but on a sliding scale of values ranging from "not passable" to "outstanding." As a matter of fact, it is possible to achieve a relatively low score without a single "incorrect" answer because of evident weakness in the qualities being measured.

Occasionally, an examination may consist entirely of an oral test – either an individual or a group oral. In such cases, information is sought concerning the technical knowledges and abilities of the candidate, since there has been no written examination for this purpose. More commonly, however, an oral test is used to supplement a written examination.

### Who conducts interviews?

The composition of oral boards varies among different jurisdictions. In nearly all, a representative of the personnel department serves as chairman. One of the members of the board may be a representative of the department in which the candidate would work. In some cases, "outside experts" are used, and, frequently, a businessman or some other representative of the general public is asked to serve. Labor and management or other special groups may be represented. The aim is to secure the services of experts in the appropriate field.

However the board is composed, it is a good idea (and not at all improper or unethical) to ascertain in advance of the interview who the members are and what groups they represent. When you are introduced to them, you will have some idea of their backgrounds and interests, and at least you will not stutter and stammer over their names.

*What should be done before the interview?*

While knowledge about the board members is useful and takes some of the surprise element out of the interview, there is other preparation which is more substantive. It *is* possible to prepare for an oral interview – in several ways:

**1) Keep a copy of your application and review it carefully before the interview**

This may be the only document before the oral board, and the starting point of the interview. Know what education and experience you have listed there, and the sequence and dates of all of it. Sometimes the board will ask you to review the highlights of your experience for them; you should not have to hem and haw doing it.

**2) Study the class specification and the examination announcement**

Usually, the oral board has one or both of these to guide them. The qualities, characteristics or knowledges required by the position sought are stated in these documents. They offer valuable clues as to the nature of the oral interview. For example, if the job involves supervisory responsibilities, the announcement will usually indicate that knowledge of modern supervisory methods and the qualifications of the candidate as a supervisor will be tested. If so, you can expect such questions, frequently in the form of a hypothetical situation which you are expected to solve. NEVER go into an oral without knowledge of the duties and responsibilities of the job you seek.

**3) Think through each qualification required**

Try to visualize the kind of questions you would ask if you were a board member. How well could you answer them? Try especially to appraise your own knowledge and background in each area, *measured against the job sought*, and identify any areas in which you are weak. Be critical and realistic – do not flatter yourself.

**4) Do some general reading in areas in which you feel you may be weak**

For example, if the job involves supervision and your past experience has NOT, some general reading in supervisory methods and practices, particularly in the field of human relations, might be useful. Do NOT study agency procedures or detailed manuals. The oral board will be testing your understanding and capacity, not your memory.

**5) Get a good night's sleep and watch your general health and mental attitude**

You will want a clear head at the interview. Take care of a cold or any other minor ailment, and of course, no hangovers.

*What should be done on the day of the interview?*

Now comes the day of the interview itself. Give yourself plenty of time to get there. Plan to arrive somewhat ahead of the scheduled time, particularly if your appointment is in the fore part of the day. If a previous candidate fails to appear, the board might be ready for you a bit early. By early afternoon an oral board is almost invariably behind schedule if there are many candidates, and you may have to wait.

Take along a book or magazine to read, or your application to review, but leave any extraneous material in the waiting room when you go in for your interview. In any event, relax and compose yourself.

The matter of dress is important. The board is forming impressions about you – from your experience, your manners, your attitude, and your appearance. Give your personal appearance careful attention. Dress your best, but not your flashiest. Choose conservative, appropriate clothing, and be sure it is immaculate. This is a business interview, and your appearance should indicate that you regard it as such. Besides, being well groomed and properly dressed will help boost your confidence.

Sooner or later, someone will call your name and escort you into the interview room. *This is it.* From here on you are on your own. It is too late for any more preparation. But remember, you asked for this opportunity to prove your fitness, and you are here because your request was granted.

*What happens when you go in?*

The usual sequence of events will be as follows: The clerk (who is often the board stenographer) will introduce you to the chairman of the oral board, who will introduce you to the other members of the board. Acknowledge the introductions before you sit down. Do not be surprised if you find a microphone facing you or a stenotypist sitting by. Oral interviews are usually recorded in the event of an appeal or other review.

Usually the chairman of the board will open the interview by reviewing the highlights of your education and work experience from your application – primarily for the benefit of the other members of the board, as well as to get the material into the record. Do not interrupt or comment unless there is an error or significant misinterpretation; if that is the case, do not hesitate. But do not quibble about insignificant matters. Also, he will usually ask you some question about your education, experience or your present job – partly to get you to start talking and to establish the interviewing "rapport." He may start the actual questioning, or turn it over to one of the other members. Frequently, each member undertakes the questioning on a particular area, one in which he is perhaps most competent, so you can expect each member to participate in the examination. Because time is limited, you may also expect some rather abrupt switches in the direction the questioning takes, so do not be upset by it. Normally, a board member will not pursue a single line of questioning unless he discovers a particular strength or weakness.

After each member has participated, the chairman will usually ask whether any member has any further questions, then will ask you if you have anything you wish to add. Unless you are expecting this question, it may floor you. Worse, it may start you off on an extended, extemporaneous speech. The board is not usually seeking more information. The question is principally to offer you a last opportunity to present further qualifications or to indicate that you have nothing to add. So, if you feel that a significant qualification or characteristic has been overlooked, it is proper to point it out in a sentence or so. Do not compliment the board on the thoroughness of their examination – they have been sketchy, and you know it. If you wish, merely say, "No thank you, I have nothing further to add." This is a point where you can "talk yourself out" of a good impression or fail to present an important bit of information. Remember, *you close the interview yourself.*

The chairman will then say, "That is all, Mr. _____, thank you." Do not be startled; the interview is over, and quicker than you think. Thank him, gather your belongings and take your leave. Save your sigh of relief for the other side of the door.

*How to put your best foot forward*

Throughout this entire process, you may feel that the board individually and collectively is trying to pierce your defenses, seek out your hidden weaknesses and embarrass and confuse you. Actually, this is not true. They are obliged to make an appraisal of your qualifications for the job you are seeking, and they want to see you in your best light. Remember, they must interview all candidates and a non-cooperative candidate may become a failure in spite of their best efforts to bring out his qualifications. Here are 15 suggestions that will help you:

**1) Be natural – Keep your attitude confident, not cocky**

If you are not confident that you can do the job, do not expect the board to be. Do not apologize for your weaknesses, try to bring out your strong points. The board is interested in a positive, not negative, presentation. Cockiness will antagonize any board member and make him wonder if you are covering up a weakness by a false show of strength.

**2) Get comfortable, but don't lounge or sprawl**

Sit erectly but not stiffly. A careless posture may lead the board to conclude that you are careless in other things, or at least that you are not impressed by the importance of the occasion. Either conclusion is natural, even if incorrect. Do not fuss with your clothing, a pencil or an ashtray. Your hands may occasionally be useful to emphasize a point; do not let them become a point of distraction.

**3) Do not wisecrack or make small talk**

This is a serious situation, and your attitude should show that you consider it as such. Further, the time of the board is limited – they do not want to waste it, and neither should you.

**4) Do not exaggerate your experience or abilities**

In the first place, from information in the application or other interviews and sources, the board may know more about you than you think. Secondly, you probably will not get away with it. An experienced board is rather adept at spotting such a situation, so do not take the chance.

**5) If you know a board member, do not make a point of it, yet do not hide it**

Certainly you are not fooling him, and probably not the other members of the board. Do not try to take advantage of your acquaintanceship – it will probably do you little good.

**6) Do not dominate the interview**

Let the board do that. They will give you the clues – do not assume that you have to do all the talking. Realize that the board has a number of questions to ask you, and do not try to take up all the interview time by showing off your extensive knowledge of the answer to the first one.

**7) Be attentive**

You only have 20 minutes or so, and you should keep your attention at its sharpest throughout. When a member is addressing a problem or question to you, give him your undivided attention. Address your reply principally to him, but do not exclude the other board members.

## 8) Do not interrupt

A board member may be stating a problem for you to analyze. He will ask you a question when the time comes. Let him state the problem, and wait for the question.

## 9) Make sure you understand the question

Do not try to answer until you are sure what the question is. If it is not clear, restate it in your own words or ask the board member to clarify it for you. However, do not haggle about minor elements.

## 10) Reply promptly but not hastily

A common entry on oral board rating sheets is "candidate responded readily," or "candidate hesitated in replies." Respond as promptly and quickly as you can, but do not jump to a hasty, ill-considered answer.

## 11) Do not be peremptory in your answers

A brief answer is proper – but do not fire your answer back. That is a losing game from your point of view. The board member can probably ask questions much faster than you can answer them.

## 12) Do not try to create the answer you think the board member wants

He is interested in what kind of mind you have and how it works – not in playing games. Furthermore, he can usually spot this practice and will actually grade you down on it.

## 13) Do not switch sides in your reply merely to agree with a board member

Frequently, a member will take a contrary position merely to draw you out and to see if you are willing and able to defend your point of view. Do not start a debate, yet do not surrender a good position. If a position is worth taking, it is worth defending.

## 14) Do not be afraid to admit an error in judgment if you are shown to be wrong

The board knows that you are forced to reply without any opportunity for careful consideration. Your answer may be demonstrably wrong. If so, admit it and get on with the interview.

## 15) Do not dwell at length on your present job

The opening question may relate to your present assignment. Answer the question but do not go into an extended discussion. You are being examined for a *new* job, not your present one. As a matter of fact, try to phrase ALL your answers in terms of the job for which you are being examined.

### Basis of Rating

Probably you will forget most of these "do's" and "don'ts" when you walk into the oral interview room. Even remembering them all will not ensure you a passing grade. Perhaps you did not have the qualifications in the first place. But remembering them will help you to put your best foot forward, without treading on the toes of the board members.

Rumor and popular opinion to the contrary notwithstanding, an oral board wants you to make the best appearance possible. They know you are under pressure – but they also want to see how you respond to it as a guide to what your reaction would be under the pressures of the job you seek. They will be influenced by the degree of poise you display, the personal traits you show and the manner in which you respond.

# EXAMINATION SECTION

# EXAMINATION SECTION
## TEST 1

DIRECTIONS: Each question or incomplete statement is followed by several suggested answers or completions. Select the one that *BEST* answers the question or completes the statement.

1. When audited financial statements are presented in a document containing other information, the auditor
   A. Has an obligation to perform auditing procedures to corroborate the other information.
   B. Is required to issue an "except for" qualified opinion if the other information has a material misstatement of fact.
   C. Should read the other information to consider whether it is inconsistent with the audited financial statements.
   D. Has **no** responsibility for the other information because it is **not** part of the basic financial statements.

1._____

2. The risk of incorrect acceptance and the risk of over-reliance on internal accounting control relate to the
   A. Preliminary estimates of materiality levels.
   B. Allowable risk of tolerable error.
   C. Efficiency of the audit.
   D. Effectiveness of the audit.

2._____

3. The expected population deviation rate of client billing errors is 3%. The auditor has established a tolerable rate of 5%. In the review of client invoices the auditor should use
   A. Stratified sampling.
   B. Variable sampling.
   C. Discovery sampling.
   D. Attribute sampling.

3._____

4. When assessing the tolerable rate, the auditor should consider that, while deviations from control procedures increase the risk of material errors, such deviations do not necessarily result in errors. This explains why
   A. A recorded disbursement that does not show evidence of required approval may nevertheless be a transaction that is properly authorized and recorded.
   B. Deviations would result in errors in the accounting records only if the deviations and the errors occurred on different transactions.
   C. Deviations from pertinent control procedures at a given rate ordinarily would be expected to result in errors at a higher rate.
   D. A recorded disbursement that is properly authorized may nevertheless be a transaction that contains a material error.

4._____

5. An auditor selects a sample from the file of shipping documents to determine whether invoices were prepared. This test is performed to satisfy the audit objective of
   A. Accuracy.
   B. Completeness.
   C. Control.
   D. Existence.

5._____

6. Which of the following departments should have the responsibility for authorizing payroll rate changes?
   A. Personnel.
   B. Payroll.
   C. Treasurer.
   D. Timekeeping.

6._____

7. An auditor would consider internal accounting control over a client's payroll procedures to be ineffective if the payroll department supervisor is responsible for
   A. Hiring subordinate payroll department employees.
   B. Having custody over unclaimed paychecks.
   C. Updating employee earnings records.
   D. Applying pay rates to time tickets.

7._____

8. For the most effective internal accounting control, monthly bank statements should be received directly from the banks and reviewed by the
   A. Controller.
   B. Cash receipts accountant.
   C. Cash disbursements accountant.
   D. Internal auditor.

8._____

9. The accountant's report expressing an opinion on an entity's system of internal accounting control should state that the
   A. Study and evaluation of the system of internal accounting control was conducted in accordance with generally accepted auditing standards.
   B. Establishment and maintenance of the system of internal accounting control are the responsibilities of management.
   C. Inherent limitations of any system of internal accounting control may prevent the preparation of financial statements in accordance with generally accepted accounting principles.
   D. Client's management has provided assurance that the expected benefits of the internal accounting control procedures are in excess of their related costs.

9._____

10. Which of the following statements is correct concerning the auditor's required communication of material weaknesses in internal accounting control?
    A. If the auditor does **not** become aware of any material weaknesses during the examination, that fact must be communicated.
    B. Weaknesses reported at interim dates should be tested for correction before completion of the engagement.
    C. Although written communication is preferable, the auditor may communicate the findings orally.
    D. Weaknesses reported at interim dates must be repeated in the communication at the completion of the engagement.

10._____

11. Which of the following internal accounting control procedures would most likely allow for a reduction in the scope of the auditor's tests of deprecation expense?
    A. Review and approval of the periodic equipment depreciation entry by a supervisor who does **not** actively participate in its preparation.
    B. Comparison of equipment account balances for the current year with the current-year budget and prior-year actual balances.
    C. Review of the miscellaneous income account for salvage credits and scrap sales of partially depreciated equipment.
    D. Authorization of payment of vendors' invoices by a designated employee who is independent of the equipment receiving function.

11._____

12. CPA firms should establish quality control policies and procedures for professional development in order to provide reasonable assurance that
    A. Employees promoted possess the appropriate characteristics to perform competently.
    B. Personnel will have the knowledge required to fulfill responsibilities assigned.
    C. The extent of supervision and review in a given instance will be appropriate.
    D. Association with a client whose management lacks integrity will be minimized.

12._____

13. An auditor generally tests physical security controls over inventory by
    A. Test counts and cutoff procedures.
    B. Examination and reconciliation.
    C. Inspection and recomputation.
    D. Inquiry and observation.

13._____

14. The most likely result of ineffective internal accounting controls in the revenue cycle is that
    A. Fictitious transactions could be recorded, causing an understatement of revenues and overstatement of receivables.
    B. Irregularities in recording transactions in the subsidiary accounts could result in a delay in goods shipped.

14._____

C. Omission of shipping documents could go undetected, causing an understatement of inventory.

D. Final authorization of credit memos by personnel in the sales department could permit an employee defalcation scheme.

15. A conceptually logical approach to the auditor's evaluation of internal accounting control consists of the following four steps:
   I. Determine whether the necessary procedures are prescribed and are being followed satisfactorily.
   II. Consider the types of errors and irregularities that could occur.
   III. Determine the internal accounting control procedures that should prevent or detect errors and irregularities.
   IV. Evaluate any weakness to determine its effect on the nature, timing, or extent of auditing procedures to be applied and suggestions to be made to the client.

What should be the order in which these four steps are performed?
   A. III, IV, I, II
   B. III, I, II, IV
   C. II, III, I, IV
   D. II, I, III, IV

15._____

16. An auditor's purpose for performing compliance testing is to provide reasonable assurance that
   A. The controls on which the auditor plans to rely are being applied as perceived during the preliminary evaluation.
   B. The risk that the auditor may unknowingly fail to modify the opinion on the financial statements is minimized.
   C. Transactions are executed in accordance with management's authorization and access to assets is limited by a segregation of functions.
   D. Transactions are recorded as necessary to permit the preparation of the financial statements in conformity with generally accepted accounting principles.

16._____

17. An auditor is **least** likely to test for compliance with the internal accounting control that provides for
   A. Segregation of the functions of recording disbursements and reconciling the bank account.
   B. Comparison of receiving reports and vendors' invoices with purchase orders.
   C. Approval of the purchase and sale of marketable securities.
   D. Classification of revenue and expense transactions by product line.

17._____

18. An auditor evaluates the existing system of internal accounting control    18._____
    primarily to
    A. Ascertain whether errors and irregularities exist.
    B. Determine the extent of compliance testing that should be performed.
    C. Determine the extent of substantive testing that should be performed.
    D. Make constructive suggestions to the client for improvement.


19. The use of fidelity bonds may indemnify a company from embezzlement    19._____
    losses. The use also
    A. Reduces the company's need to obtain expensive business interruption
       insurance.
    B. Protects employees who made unintentional errors from possible
       monetary damages resulting from such errors.
    C. Allows the company to substitute the fidelity bonds for various parts of
       internal accounting control.
    D. Reduces the possibility of employing persons with dubious records in
       positions of trust.


20. Inquiry and analytical procedures ordinarily performed during a review of a    20._____
    nonpublic entity's financial statements include
    A. Analytical procedures designed to identify material weaknesses in internal
       accounting control.
    B. Inquiries concerning actions taken at meetings of the stockholders and
       the board of directors.
    C. Analytical procedures designed to test the accounting records by
       obtaining corroborating evidential matter.
    D. Inquiries of knowledgeable outside parties such as the client's attorneys
       and bankers.


21. An accountant has been asked to issue a review report on the balance sheet    21._____
    of a nonpublic company but not to report on the other basic financial
    statements. The accountant may **not** do so
    A. Because compliance with this request would result in an incomplete
       review.
    B. Because compliance with this request would result in a violation of the
       ethical standards of the profession.
    C. If the scope of the inquiry an analytical procedures has been restricted.
    D. If the review of the balance sheet discloses material departures from
       generally accepted accounting principles.

22. While substantive tests may support the accuracy of underlying records, these tests frequently provide **no** affirmative evidence of segregation of duties because

    22._____

    A. Substantive tests rarely guarantee the accuracy of the records if only a sample of the transactions has been tested.

    B. The records may be accurate even though they are maintained by persons having incompatible functions.

    C. Substantive tests relate to the entire period under audit, but compliance tests ordinarily are confined to the period during which the auditor is on the client's premises.

    D. Many computerized procedures leave **no** audit trail of who performed them, so substantive tests may necessarily be limited to inquiries and observation of office personnel.

23. Hill has decided to use Probability Proportional to Size (PPS) sampling, sometimes called dollar-unit sampling, in the audit of a client's accounts receivable balances. Hill plans to use the following PPS sampling table:

    23._____

### TABLE
### Reliability Factors for Errors of Overstatement

| Number of over-statement errors | Risk of Incorrect Acceptance | | | | |
|---|---|---|---|---|---|
| | 1% | 5% | 10% | 15% | 20% |
| 0 | 4.61 | 3.00 | 2.31 | 1.90 | 1.61 |
| 1 | 6.64 | 4.75 | 3.89 | 3.38 | 3.00 |
| 2 | 8.41 | 6.30 | 5.33 | 4.72 | 4.28 |
| 3 | 10.05 | 7.76 | 6.69 | 6.02 | 5.52 |
| 4 | 11.61 | 9.16 | 8.00 | 7.27 | 6.73 |

### Additional Information

Tolerable error
    (net of effect of expected error).................................................................$24,000
Risk of incorrect acceptance .........................................................................20%
Number of errors allowed................................................................................1
Recorded amount of accounts receivable ...............................................$240,000
Number of accounts .....................................................................................360

What sample size should Hill use?
    A. 120
    B. 108
    C. 60
    D. 30

24. An auditor's program for the examination of long-term debt should include steps that require the     24._____
 A. Inspection of the accounts payable subsidiary ledger.
 B. Investigation of credits to the bond interest income account.
 C. Verification of the existence of the bondholders.
 D. Examination of any bond trust indenture.

25. An attorney responding to an auditor as a result of the client's letter of audit inquiry may appropriately limit the response to     25._____
 A. Items which have high probability of being resolved to the client's detriment.
 B. Asserted claims and pending or threatened litigation.
 C. Legal matters subject to unsettled points of law, uncorroborated information, or other complex judgments.
 D. Matters to which the attorney has given substantive attention in the form of legal consultation or representation.

26. Which of the following statements ordinarily is included among the written client representations obtained by the auditor?     26._____
 A. Sufficient evidential matter has been made available to permit the issuance of an unqualified opinion.
 B. Compensating balances and other arrangements involving restrictions on cash balances have been disclosed.
 C. Management acknowledges responsibility for illegal actions committed by employees.
 D. Management acknowledges that there are **no** material weaknesses in internal accounting controls.

27. After accounting for a sequence of inventory tags, an auditor traces a sample     27._____

 of tags to the physical inventory listing to obtain evidence that all items
 A. Included in the listing have been counted.
 B. Represented by inventory tags are included in the listing.
 C. Included in the listing are represented by inventory tags.
 D. Represented by inventory tags are bona fide.

28. One reason why an auditor makes an analytical review of the client's operations is to identify     28._____
 A. Improper separation of accounting and other financial duties.
 B. Weaknesses of a material nature in the system of internal accounting control.
 C. Unusual transactions.
 D. Non-compliance with prescribed control procedures.

29. When considering the use of management's written representations as audit evidence about the completeness assertion, an auditor should understand that such representations
    A. Complement, but do **not** replace, substantive tests designed to support the assertion.
    B. Constitute sufficient evidence to support the assertion when considered in combination with reliance on internal accounting controls.
    C. Are not part of the evidential matter considered to support the assertion.
    D. Replace reliance on internal accounting controls as evidence to support the assertion.

29._____

30. An audit working paper that reflects the major components of an amount reported in the financial statements is referred to as a(an)
    A. Lead schedule.
    B. Supporting schedule.
    C. Audit control account.
    D. Working trial balance.

30._____

---

# KEY (CORRECT ANSWERS)

| | |
|---|---|
| 1. C | 16. A |
| 2. D | 17. D |
| 3. D | 18. C |
| 4. A | 19. D |
| 5. B | 20. B |
| | |
| 6. A | 21. C |
| 7. B | 22. B |
| 8. D | 23. D |
| 9. B | 24. D |
| 10. C | 25. D |
| | |
| 11. A | 26. B |
| 12. B | 27. B |
| 13. D | 28. C |
| 14. D | 29. A |
| 15. C | 30. A |

---

# TEST 2

DIRECTIONS: Each question or incomplete statement is followed by several suggested answers or completions. Select the one that *BEST* answers the question or completes the statement.

1. The underwriter of a securities offering may request that an auditor perform specified procedures and supply certain assurances concerning unaudited information contained in a registration statement. The auditor's response to such a request is commonly called a
   A. Report under federal security statutes.
   B. Comfort letter.
   C. Review of interim financial information.
   D. Compilation report for underwriters.

1._____

2. A CPA should **not** submit unaudited financial statements of a nonpublic company to a client or others unless, as a minimum, the CPA complies with the provisions applicable to
   A. Compulation engagements.
   B. Review engagements.
   C. Statements on auditing standards.
   D. Attestation standards.

2._____

3. The most likely explanation why the auditor's examination **cannot** reasonably be expected to bring all illegal acts by the client to the auditor's attention is that
   A. Illegal acts are perpetrated by management override of internal accounting controls.
   B. Illegal acts by clients often relate to operating aspects rather than accounting aspects.
   C. The client's system of internal accounting control may be so strong that the auditor performs only minimal substantive testing.
   D. Illegal acts may be perpetrated by the only person in the client's organization with access to both assets and the accounting records.

3._____

4. As lower acceptable levels of both audit risk and materiality are established, the auditor should plan more work on individual accounts to
   A. Find smaller errors.
   B. Find larger errors.
   C. Increase the tolerable error in the accounts.
   D. Decrease the risk of overreliance.

4._____

5. The element of the audit planning process most likely to be agreed upon with the client before implementation of the audit strategy is the determination of the
   A. Methods of statistical sampling to be used in confirming accounts receivable.
   B. Pending legal matters to be included in the inquiry of the client's attorney.
   C. Evidence to be gathered to provide a sufficient basis for the auditor's opinion.
   D. Schedules and analyses to be prepared by the client's staff.

   5._____

6. With respect to errors and irregularities, the auditor should plan to
   A. Search for errors that would have a material effect and for irregularities that would have either material or immaterial effect on the financial statements.
   B. Search for irregularities that would have a material effect and for errors that would have either material or immaterial effect on the financial statements.
   C. Search for errors or irregularities that would have a material effect on the financial statements.
   D. Discover errors or irregularities that have either material or immaterial effect on the financial statements.

   6._____

7. Because an examination in accordance with generally accepted auditing standards is influenced by the possibility of material errors, the auditor should conduct the examination with an attitude of
   A. Professional responsiveness.
   B. Conservative advocacy.
   C. Objective judgment.
   D. Professional skepticism.

   7._____

8. The risk that an auditor's procedures will lead to the conclusion that a material error does **not** exist in an account balance when, in fact, such error does exist is referred to as
   A. Audit risk.
   B. Inherent risk.
   C. Control risk.
   D. Detection risk.

   8._____

9. Which one of the following is an enforceable set of pronouncements of an authoritative body designated to establish accounting principles, according to the AICPA Code of Professional Ethics?
   A. AICPA Statements on Standards for Accounting and Review Services.
   B. AICPA Statements of Position.
   C. FASB Interpretations.
   D. FASB Statements of Financial Accounting Concepts.

   9._____

10. According to the AICPA Code of Professional Ethics, may a CPA who is in partnership with non-CPAs sign a report with the firm name and below it affix the CPA's own signature with the designation "Certified Public Accountant"?
    A. No, because a CPA should **not** form a partnership with non-CPAs.
    B. No, because it would appear that all partners were associated with the report when only one actually is associated.
    C. Yes, provided the non-CPA partners adhere to the professional standards concerning quality control.
    D. Yes, provided it is clear that the partnership itself is **not** being held out as composed entirely of CPAs.

10._____

11. In planning a new engagement, which of the following is **not** a factor that affects the auditor's judgment as to the quantity, type, and content of working papers?
    A. The auditor's estimated occurrence rate of attributes.
    B. The auditor's preliminary evaluations of risk based on discussions with the client.
    C. The content of the client's representation letter.
    D. The type of report to be issued by the auditor.

11._____

12. An auditor strives to achieve independence in appearance in order to
    A. Maintain public confidence in the profession.
    B. Become independent in fact.
    C. Comply with the generally accepted auditing standards of field work.
    D. Maintain an unbiased mental attitude.

12._____

13. If requested to perform a review engagement for a nonpublic entity in which an accountant has an immaterial direct financial interest, the accountant is
    A. Not independent and, therefore, may issue a review report, but may **not** issue an auditor's opinion.
    B. Not independent and, therefore, may **not** issue a review report.
    C. Not independent and, therefore, may **not** be associated with the financial statements.
    D. Independent because the financial interest is immaterial and, therefore, may issue a review report.

13._____

14. Audits of certain governmental entities are required to be performed in accordance with generally accepted government auditing standards (GAGAS). These standards do **not** require, as part of an auditor's report, the identification of
    A. Significant internal accounting and administrative controls designed to provide reasonable assurance that federal programs are being administered in compliance with applicable laws and regulations.
    B. Material weaknesses discovered as a result of the study and evaluation of the internal control systems.

14._____

C. Sampling methods used to test the internal controls designed to detect errors and irregularities.

D. Significant internal accounting and administrative controls that were **not** evaluated, and the reasons why they were **not** evaluated.

15. A flowchart is most frequently used by an auditor in connection with the        15._____
    A. Preparation of generalized computer audit programs.
    B. Review of the client's internal accounting controls.
    C. Use of statistical sampling in performing an audit.
    D. Performance of analytical review procedures of account balances.

16. Which of the following statements is correct regarding the auditor's        16._____
responsibilities for supplementary information required by the FASB?
    A. Because the supplementary information is a required part of the basic financial statements, the auditor should apply normal auditing procedures.
    B. The omission of, but **not** deficiencies in, supplementary information should be disclosed in the opinion paragraph of the auditor's report.
    C. Because the supplementary information is **not** a required part of the basic financial statements, the auditor should apply only certain limited procedures.
    D. The omission of supplementary information ordinarily requires the auditor to issue an adverse opinion, but mere deficiencies require an "except for" qualified opinion.

17. Baker, the continuing auditor of AC Resources, a publicly held company, has        17._____
been requested to report on the system of internal accounting control. The report is to be based solely on the study and evaluation of internal accounting control that Baker made in the audit of AC's financial statements, even though the study and evaluation is not sufficient for expressing an opinion on the system taken as a whole. Baker intends to describe the limited purpose of the study and evaluation and to disclaim an opinion on the system taken as a whole. In these circumstances, Baker
    A. May report provided the report indicates it is intended solely for management or other specified parties.
    B. May report provided the report is included with the basic financial statements distributed to the stockholders.
    C. May **not** report because there is **no** basis for determining whether material errors or irregularities may occur and be detected.
    D. May **not** report because it would be a violation of generally accepted auditing standards.

18. In which of the following reports should an accountant not express negative or limited assurance?
    A. A standard review report on financial statements of a nonpublic entity.
    B. A standard compilation report on financial statements of a nonpublic entity.
    C. A standard comfort letter on financial information included in a registration statement of a public entity.
    D. A standard review report on interim financial statements of a public entity.

18._____

19. The party responsible for assumptions identified in the preparation of prospective financial statements is usually
    A. A third-party lending institution.
    B. The client's management.
    C. The reporting accountant.
    D. The client's independent auditor.

19._____

20. Which of the following is a prospective financial statement for general use upon which an accountant may appropriately report?
    A. Financial projection.
    B. Partial presentation.
    C. Pro forma financial statement.
    D. Financial forecast.

20._____

21. When third party use of prospective financial statements is expected, an accountant may **not** accept an engagement to
    A. Perform a review.
    B. Perform a compilation.
    C. Perform an examination.
    D. Apply agreed-upon procedures.

21._____

22. An auditor's report on financial statements prepared in accordance with a comprehensive basis of accounting other than generally accepted accounting principles should include all of the following **except**
    A. Reference to the note to the financial statements that describes how the basis of preparation differs from generally accepted accounting principles.
    B. Disclosure of the fact that the financial statements are **not** intended to be presented in conformity with generally accepted accounting principles.
    C. An opinion as to whether the basis of accounting used is appropriate under the circumstances.
    D. An opinion as to whether the financial statements are presented fairly in conformity with the basis of accounting described.

22._____

23. If the auditor believes that financial statements prepared on the entity's income tax basis are **not** suitably titled, the auditor should
    A. Issue a disclaimer of opinion.
    B. Explain in the notes to the financial statements the terminology used.
    C. Issue a compilation report.
    D. Modify the auditor's report to disclose any reservations.

23._____

24. Financial statements compiled without audit or review by an accountant should be accompanied by a report stating that
    A. The financial statements have **not** been audited or reviewed and, accordingly, the accountant expresses only limited assurance on them.
    B. A compilation is limited to presenting in the form of financial statements information that is the representation of management.
    C. The accountant is **not** aware of any material modifications that should be made to the financial statements for them to conform with generally accepted accounting principles.
    D. A compilation is less in scope than a review, and substantially less in scope than an examination in accordance with generally accepted auditing standards.

24.__B__

25. An auditor who is determining the scope of work to be performed concerning possible related party transactions should
    A. Assume that transactions with related parties are outside the ordinary course of business.
    B. Determine whether transactions with related parties would have taken place if the parties had **not** been related.
    C. Obtain an understanding of management responsibilities and the relationship of each of the parties to the total entity.
    D. Establish a basis of accounting principles different from that which would have been appropriate had the parties **not** been related.

25._____

26. The prior year's financial statements of YZ, Inc., which were audited by Pate, CPA, are presented for comparative purposes without Pate's audit report. Jennings, CPA, the successor auditor, should indicate in the current year audit report that the prior year's financial statements were examined by another auditor
    A. Only if Pate's opinion was other than unqualified.
    B. But should **not** indicate the type of opinion expressed by Pate.
    C. Only if the prior year's financial statements have been restated.
    D. But should **not** name Pate as the predecessor auditor.

26._____

27. The objective of auditing procedures applied to segment information is to provide the auditor with a reasonable basis for concluding whether
    A. The information is useful for comparing a segment of one enterprise with a similar segment of another enterprise.
    B. Sufficient evidential matter has been obtained to allow the auditor to be associated with the segment information.
    C. A separate opinion on the segment information is necessary due to inconsistent application of accounting principles.
    D. The information is presented in conformity with the FASB Statement on segment information in relation to the financial statements taken as a whole.

27._____

28. For which of the following events would the auditor appropriately issue a report that contains the standard phrase concerning consistency?
    A. A change in the percentage used to calculate the provision for warranty expense.
    B. Correction of a mistake in the application of a generally accepted accounting principle.
    C. A change in the method of accounting for specific subsidiaries that constitute the group of companies for which consolidated statements are presented.
    D. A change from an accounting principle that is **not** generally accepted to one that is generally accepted.

28. __A__

29. When a question arises about an entity's continued existence, the auditor should consider factors tending to mitigate the significance of contrary information concerning the entity's alternative means for maintaining adequate cash flow. An example of such a factor is the
    A. Possibility of purchasing certain assets rather than leasing them.
    B. Capability of extending the due dates of existing loans.
    C. Feasibility of operating at increased levels of production.
    D. Marketability of property and equipment that management plans to keep.

29._____

30. An auditor has been asked to report on the balance sheet of Kane Company but not on the other basic financial statements. The auditor will have access to al information underlying the basic financial statements. Under these circumstances, the auditor
    A. May accept the engagement because such engagements merely involve limited reporting objectives.
    B. May accept the engagement but should disclaim an opinion because of an inability to apply the procedures considered necessary.
    C. Should refuse the engagement because there is a client-imposed scope limitation.
    D. Should refuse the engagement because of a departure from generally accepted auditing standards.

30.__A__

# KEY (CORRECT ANSWERS)

| | |
|---|---|
| 1. B | 16. C |
| 2. A | 17. A |
| 3. B | 18. B |
| 4. A | 19. B |
| 5. D | 20. D |
| | |
| 6. C | 21. A |
| 7. D | 22. C |
| 8. D | 23. D |
| 9. C | 24. B |
| 10. D | 25. C |
| | |
| 11. C | 26. D |
| 12. A | 27. D |
| 13. B | 28. A |
| 14. C | 29. B |
| 15. B | 30. A |

# TEST 1

DIRECTIONS:
Each question or incomplete statement is followed by several suggested answers or completions. Select the one that *BEST* answers the question or completes the statement. *PRINT THE LETTER OF THE CORRECT ANSWER IN THE SPACE AT THE RIGHT.*

1. The use of a disclaimer of opinion might indicate that the auditor        1. ...
    A. is so uncertain with respect to an item that he cannot form an opinion on the fairness of presentation of the financial statements as a whole
    B. is uncertain with respect to an item that is material but not so material that he cannot form an opinion on the fairness of presentation of the financial statements as a whole
    C. has observed a violation of generally accepted accounting principles that has a material effect upon the fairness of presentation of financial statements, but is not so material that a qualified report is unjustified
    D. has observed a violation of generally accepted accounting principles that is so material that a qualified opinion is not justified

2. An auditor's "subject to" report is a type of        2. ...
    A. disclaimer of opinion      B. qualified opinion
    C. adverse opinion           D. standard opinion

3. An accountant will issue an adverse auditor's opinion if        3. ...
    A. the scope of his examination is limited by the client
    B. his exception to the fairness of presentation is so material that an "except for" opinion is not justified
    C. he did not perform sufficient auditing procedures to form an opinion on the financial statements taken as a whole
    D. such major uncertainties exist concerning the company's future that a "subject to" opinion is not justified

4. An auditor will express an "except for" opinion if        4. ...
    A. the client refuses to provide for a probable federal income tax deficiency that is material
    B. the degree of uncertainty associated with the client company's future makes a "subject to" opinion inappropriate
    C. he did not perform procedures sufficient to form an opinion on the consistency of application of generally accepted accounting principles
    D. he is basing his opinion in part upon work done by another auditor

5. Carl Sanborn, accountant, provides bookkeeping services to Alamo Products Co. He also is a director of Alamo and performs limited auditing procedures in connection with his preparation of Alamo's financial statements. Sanborn's report accompanying these financial statements should include a        5. ...
    A. detailed description of the limited auditing procedures performed

    B. complete description of the relationships with
       Alamo that imperil Sanborn's independence
    C. disclaimer of opinion and statement that financial
       statements are unaudited on each page of the finan-
       cial statements
    D. qualified opinion because of his lack of independence
       together with such assurance as his limited auditing
       procedures can provide

6. It was impracticable for an accountant to observe the     6. ...
physical inventory that his client conducted on the
balance-sheet date.  The accountant satisfied himself
as to inventory quantities by other procedures.  These
procedures included making some physical counts of the
inventory a week later and applying appropriate tests to
intervening transactions.
In his report on the financial statements, the accountant
    A. must disclose the modification of the scope of his
       examination and express a qualified opinion
    B. must disclose the modification of the scope of his
       examination, but may express an unqualified opinion
    C. may omit reference to any modification of the scope
       of his examination and express an unqualified opinion
    D. may omit reference to modification of the scope of
       his examination only if he describes the circumstances
       in an  explanatory paragraph or his opinion paragraph

7. In connection with his examination of the financial state- 7. ...
ments of San Diego Co., an accountant is unable to form an
opinion as to the proper statement of several accounts.
A piecemeal opinion may  be appropriate if
    A. the accounts in question are immaterial in terms of
       San Diego's financial position and results of opera-
       tions
    B. the failure to form an opinion is the result of re-
       strictions imposed by the client
    C. the piecemeal opinion is accompanied by a qualified
       opinion on the financial statements taken as a whole
    D. in the auditor's judgment, the piecemeal opinion will
       serve a useful purpose

8. On its business stationery, an accounting firm should *NOT* 8. ...
list
    A. the firm's name, address, and telephone number
    B. names of deceased partners in the firm name
    C. membership in state accounting society
    D. that it has tax expertise

9. An accountant should *reject* a management advisory ser- 9. ...
vices engagement if
    A. it would require him to make management decisions
       for an audit client
    B. his recommendations are to be subject to review by
       the client
    C. he audits the financial statements of a subsidiary
       of the prospective client
    D. the proposed engagement is not accounting-related

10. When an accountant lacks independence in connection with an audit engagement, he should          10. ...
    A. state, in his auditor's report, the reason for his lack of independence
    B. disclaim an opinion on the financial statements
    C. list, in his auditor's report, all the generally accepted auditing procedures actually performed by him
    D. issue a piecemeal opinion

11. Tozzi, an accountant, has a small public accounting practice. One of Tozzi's clients desires services which Tozzi cannot adequately provide. Tozzi has recommended a larger firm, Casso & Co., to his client, and, in return, Casso has agreed to pay Tozzi 10% of the fee for services rendered by Casso for Tozzi's client. Who, if anyone, is in violation of the AICPA's Code of Professional Ethics?          11. ...
    A. *Both* Tozzi and Casso          B. *Neither* Tozzi nor Casso
    C. *Only* Tozzi          D. *Only* Casso

12. The accountant who regularly examines Venus Corporation's financial statements has been asked to prepare pro forma income statements for the next five years. If the statements are to be based upon the Corporation's operating assumptions and are for internal use only, the accountant should          12. ...
    A. *reject* the engagement because the statements are to be based upon assumptions
    B. *reject* the engagement because the statements are for internal use
    C. *accept* the engagement provided full disclosure is made of the assumptions used and the extent of the accountant's responsibility
    D. *accept* the engagement provided Venus certifies in writing that the statements are for internal use only

13. For purposes of expressing a piecemeal opinion, the threshold of materiality ordinarily is          13. ...
    A. *higher* (i.e., larger amounts are immaterial) because the auditor is not expressing an overall opinion on financial position and the results of operations
    B. *lower* (i.e., smaller amounts are material) because the individual items stand alone, thus affording a smaller base
    C. *unchanged* from the threshold that the auditor would use in expressing an overall opinion on financial position and the results of operations
    D. *not applicable* because piecemeal opinions may be used only for accounts that are subject to fairly exact quantification

14. In forming his opinion upon the consolidated financial statements of Saturn Corp., an accountant relies upon another auditor's examination of the financial statements of Io, Inc., a wholly owned subsidiary whose operations constitute 30% of Saturn's consolidated total. Io's auditor expresses an unqualified opinion on that company's financial statements.          14. ...

The accountant examining Saturn Corp. may be expected to express an unqualified opinion but refer to the report by the other auditor if he

- A. concludes, based upon a review of the other auditor's professional standing and qualifications, that he is willing to assume the same responsibility as though he had performed the audit of Io's financial statements himself
- B. is satisfied with the audit scope for the subsidiary, based upon his review of the audit program, but his inquiries disclose that the other auditor is not independent or lacks professional standing
- C. is satisfied with the other auditor's professional standing but concludes, based upon a review of the audit program, that the audit scope for the examination of Io's financial statements was inadequate
- D. is satisfied with the other auditor's professional reputation and audit scope but is unwilling to assume responsibility for the other auditor's work to the same extent as though he had performed the work himself

15. If a principal auditor decides that he will refer in his report to the examination of another auditor, he is required to disclose the    15. ...

- A. name of the other auditor
- B. nature of his inquiry into the other auditor's professional standing and extent of his review of the other auditor's work
- C. portion of the financial statements examined by the other auditor
- D. reasons why he is unwilling to assume responsibility for the other auditor's work

16. On August 15, 1985, an accountant completed field work    16. ...
on an examination of the financial statements of the Wyoming Corporation for the year ended June 30, 1985. On September 1, 1985, before issuance of the accountant's report on the financial statements, an event occurred that the accountant and Wyoming agree should be incorporated by footnote in the financial statements for the year ended June 30, 1985. The accountant has not otherwise reviewed events subsequent to the completion of field work.
The accountant's report should be dated

- A. September 1
- B. June 30, except for the footnote, which should be dated September 1
- C. August 15
- D. August 15, except for the footnote, which should be dated September 1

17. In performing a review of his client's cash disbursements, an accountant uses systematic sampling with a random start.    17. ...
The *PRIMARY* disadvantage of systematic sampling is that population items

A. must be reordered in a systematic pattern before the sample can be drawn
B. may occur in a systematic pattern, thus negating the randomness of the sample
C. may occur twice in the sample
D. must be replaced in the population after sampling to permit valid statistical inference

18. From prior experience, an accountant is aware of the fact that cash disbursements contain a few unusually large disbursements.
    In using statistical sampling, the accountant's *BEST* course of action is to
    A. *eliminate* any unusually large disbursements which appear in the sample
    B. *continue* to draw new samples until no unusually large disbursements appear in the sample
    C. *stratify* the cash-disbrusements population so that the unusually large disbursements are reviewed separately
    D. *increase* the sample size to lessen the effect of the unusually large disbursements

18. ...-

19. In connection with his test of the accuracy of inventory counts, an accountant decides to use discovery sampling.
    Discovery sampling may be considered a special case of
    A. judgmental sampling     B. sampling for variables
    C. stratified sampling     D. sampling for attributes

19. ...

20. An accountant's test of the accuracy of inventory counts involves two storehouses. Storehouse A contains 10,000 inventory items and Storehouse B contains 5,000 items. The accountant plans to use sampling without replacement to test for an estimated 5% error rate.
    If the accountant's sampling plan calls for a specified reliability of 95% and a maximum tolerable error occurrence rate of 7.5% for both storehouses, the ratio of the size of the accountant's sample from Storehouse A to the size of the sample from Storehouse B should be
    A. more than 1:1 but less than 2:1
    B. 2:1                 C. 1:1
    D. more than .5:1 but less than 1:1

20. ...

_____

# KEY (CORRECT ANSWERS)

| | | | |
|---|---|---|---|
| 1. A | | 11. B | |
| 2. B | | 12. C | |
| 3. B | | 13. B | |
| 4. A | | 14. D | |
| 5. C | | 15. C | |
| | | | |
| 6. C | | 16. D | |
| 7. D | | 17. B | |
| 8. D | | 18. C | |
| 9. A | | 19. D | |
| 10. B | | 20. A | |

_____

# TEST 2

DIRECTIONS:
    Each question or incomplete statement is followed by several suggested answers or completions. Select the one that *BEST* answers the question or completes the statement. *PRINT THE LETTER OF THE CORRECT ANSWER IN THE SPACE AT THE RIGHT.*

1. Approximately 5% of the 10,000 homogeneous items included in Barrow's finished-goods inventory are believed to be defective. The accountant examining Barrow's financial statements decides to test this estimated 5% defective rate. He learns that, by sampling without replacement, a sample of 284 items from the inventory will permit specified reliability (confidence level) of 95% and specified precision (confidence interval) of $\pm$ .025.
    If specified precision is changed to $\pm$ .05, and specified reliability remains 95%, the required sample size is
    A. 72        B. 335        C. 436        D. 1,543

1. ... A

2. The "reliability" (confidence level) of an estimate made from sample data is a mathematically determined figure that expresses the expected proportion of possible samples of a specified size from a given population
    A. that will yield an interval estimate that will encompass the true population value
    B. that will yield an interval estimate that will not encompass the true population value
    C. for which the sample value and the population value are identical
    D. for which the sample elements will not exceed the population elements by more than a stated amount

2. ... A

3. In an examination of financial statements, an accountant generally will find stratified-sampling techniques to be *LEAST* appropriate to
    A. examining charges to the maintenance account during the audit year
    B. tests of transactions for compliance with internal control
    C. the recomputation of a sample of factory-workers' net pay
    D. year-end confirmation of bank balances

3. ... D

4. An accountant's client wishes to determine inventory shrinkage by weighing a sample of inventory items. If a stratified random sample is to be drawn, the strata should be identified in such a way that
    A. the overall population is divided into subpopulations of equal size so that each subpopulation can be given equal weight when estimates are made
    B. each stratum differs as much as possible with respect to expected shrinkage but the shrinkages expected for items within each stratum are as close as possible
    C. the sample mean and standard deviation of each individual stratum will be equal to the means and standard deviations of all other strata

4. ... B

    D. the items in each stratum will follow a normal
       distribution so that probability theory can be
       used in making inferences from the sample data
5. In estimating the total value of supplies on repair          5. *B*
   trucks, Breaker Company draws random samples from two
   equal-sized strata of trucks. The mean value of the
   inventory stored on the larger trucks (stratum 1) was
   computed at $1,500, with a standard deviation of $250.
   On the smaller trucks (stratum 2), the mean value of
   inventory was computed as $500, with a standard devia-
   tion of $45.
   If Breaker had drawn an unstratified sample from the
   entire population of trucks, the expected mean value of
   inventory per truck would be $1,000, and the expected
   standard deviation would be
    A. *exactly* $147.50            B. *greater* than $250
    C. *less* than $45
    D. *between* $45 and $250, but not $147.50
6. An accountant conducting his first examination of the        6. *A*
   financial statements of Goldfang Corporation, is considering the propriety of reducing his work by consulting with the predecessor auditor and reviewing the predecessor's working papers.
   This procedure is
    A. acceptable
    B. required if the new auditor is to render an un-
       qualified opinion
    C. acceptable only if the accountant refers in his
       report to his reliance upon the predecessor auditor's
       work
    D. unacceptable because the accountant should bring an
       independent viewpoint to a new engagement
7. The statement that *BEST* expresses the auditor's respon-    7. *D*
   sibility with respect to events occurring between the
   balance-sheet date and the end of his examination is that
   the
    A. auditor has no responsibility for events occurring
       in the subsequent period unless these events affect
       transactions recorded on or before the balance-sheet
       date
    B. auditor's responsibility is to determine that a
       proper cutoff has been made and that transactions
       recorded on or before the balance-sheet date actual-
       ly occurred
    C. auditor is fully responsible for events occurring
       in the subsequent period and should extend all de-
       tailed procedures through the last day of field work
    D. auditor is responsible for determining that a proper
       cutoff has been made and performing a general review
       of events occurring in the subsequent period
8. An auditor's unqualified short-form report                   8. *B*
    A. *implies* only that items disclosed in the financial
       statements and footnotes are properly presented and
       takes no position on the adequacy of disclosure

B. *implies* that disclosure is adequate in the financial statements and footnotes

C. *explicitly* states that disclosure is adequate in the financial statements and footnotes

D. *explicitly* states that all material items have been disclosed in conformity with generally accepted accounting principles

9. An accountant is completing his examination of the financial statements of the Jupiter Service Company for the year ended April 30, 1985. During the year, Jupiter's employees were granted an additional week's vacation, and this had a material effect upon vacation pay expense for the year and the accrued liability for vacation-pay at April 30, 1985. In the opinion of the accountant, this occurrence and its effects have been adequately disclosed in a footnote to the financial statements. In his auditor's report, the accountant *normally* will:

A. Omit any mention of this occurrence and its effects

B. Refer to the footnote in his opinion paragraph but express an unqualified opinion

C. Refer to the footnote and express an opinion that is qualified as to consistency

D. Insist that comparative income statements for prior years be restated or express an opinion that is qualified as to consistency

9. ... A

10. While assisting Tension Co. in the preparation of un-audited financial statements, Walter Lamb, accountant, noted that Tension had increased property, plant, and equipment to reflect a recent property appraisal. In this circumstance, Mr. Lamb's reporting responsibility is met by

A. issuing the statements on plain paper without reference to the accountant

B. advising Tension's management of the deviation from generally accepted accounting principles

C. describing the deviation from generally accepted accounting principles in his disclaimer of opinion

D. stating in his disclaimer of opinion that Tension's financial statements are unaudited

10. ... C

11. The *PRIMARY* responsibility for the adequacy of disclosure in the financial statements and footnotes rests with the

A. partner assigned to the engagement

B. auditor in charge of field work

C. staffman who drafts the statements and footnotes

D. client

11. ... D

12. The use of an adverse opinion *generally* indicates:

A. *Uncertainty* with respect to an item that is so material that the auditor cannot form an opinion on the fairness of presentation of the financial statements as a whole

B. *Uncertainty* with respect to an item that is material but not so material that the auditor cannot form an opinion on the fairness of the financial statements as a whole

12. ... D

   C. *A violation* of generally accepted accounting prin-
      ciples that has a material effect upon the fairness
      of presentation of the financial statements, but is
      not so material that a qualified opinion is unjusti-
      fied
   D. *A violation* of generally accepted accounting prin-
      ciples that is so material that a qualified opinion
      is not justified

13. Purdue Sales Company asked an accountant's assistance          13. B
    in planning the use of multiple regression analysis to
    predict district sales. An equation has been estimated
    based upon historical data, and a standard error has been
    computed.
    When regression analysis based upon past periods is used
    to predict for a future period, the standard error associ-
    ated with the predicted value, in relation to the standard
    error for the base equation, will be
       A. smaller           B. larger              C. the same
       D. larger or smaller, depending upon the circumstances

14. An accountant's client maintains perpetual inventory           14. A
    records. In the past, all inventory items have been
    counted on a cycle basis at least once during the year.
    Physical count and perpetual record differences have been
    minor. Now, the client wishes to minimize the cost of
    physically counting the inventory by changing to a sampling
    method in which many inventory items will not be counted
    during a given year.
    For purposes of expressing an opinion on his client's
    financial statements, the accountant will accept the
    sampling method *only* if
       A. the sampling method has statistical validity
       B. a stratified sampling plan is used
       C. the client is willing to accept an opinion
          qualification in the auditor's report
       D. the client is willing to accept a scope quali-
          fication in the auditor's report

15. Returns of positive-confirmation requests for accounts         15. B
    receivable were very poor. As an alternative procedure,
    the auditor decided to check subsequent collections.
    The auditor had satisfied himself that the client satis-
    factorily listed the customer name next to each check
    listed on the deposit slip; hence, he decided that,for
    each customer for which a confirmation was not received,
       he would add all amounts shown for that customer on
    each validated deposit slip for the two months following
    the balance-sheet date.
    The *MAJOR* fallacy in the auditor's procedure is that
       A. checking of subsequent collections is not an ac-
          cepted alternative auditing procedure for confirma-
          tion of accounts receivable
       B. by looking only at the deposit slip, the auditor
          would not know whether the payment was for the re-
          ceivable at the balance-sheet data or a subsequent
          transaction

9

C. the deposit slip would not be received directly by the auditor as a confirmation would be

D. a customer may not have made a payment during the two-month period

16. Cherry Company, whose financial statements are unaudited, has engaged an accountant to make a special review and report on Cherry's internal accounting control. In general, to which of the following will this report be *LEAST* useful? 16. ...

    A. Cherry's management

    B. Present and prospective customers

    C. A regulatory agency having jurisdiction over Cherry

    D. The independent auditor of Cherry's parent company

17. Lapping would *MOST* likely be detected by 17. ...

    A. examination of canceled checks clearing in the bank-cutoff period

    B. confirming year-end bank balances

    C. preparing a schedule of interbank transfers

    D. investigating responses to account-receivable confirmations

18. From the standpoint of good procedural control, distributing payroll checks to employees is *BEST* handled by the 18. ...

    A. accounting department    B. personnel department

    C. treasurer's department

    D. employee's departmental supervisor

19. In a company whose materials and supplies include a great number of items, a *fundamental* deficiency in control requirements would be indicated if 19. ...

    A. perpetual inventory records were not maintained for items of small value

    B. the storekeeping function were to be combined with production and record-keeping

    C. the cycle basis for physical inventory taking were to be used

    D. minor supply items were to be expensed when purchased

20. In violation of company policy, the Monroe City Company erroneously capitalized the cost of painting its warehouse. The accountant examining Monroe City's financial statements *MOST* likely would learn of this by 20. ...

    A. *reviewing* the listing of construction work orders for the year

    B. *discussing* capitalization policies with the company controller

    C. *observing*, during his physical inventory observation, that the warehouse had been painted

    D. *examining* in detail a sample of construction work orders

## KEY (CORRECT ANSWERS)

| | | | |
|---|---|---|---|
| 1. A | 6. A | 11. D | 16. B |
| 2. A | 7. D | 12. D | 17. D |
| 3. D | 8. B | 13. B | 18. C |
| 4. B | 9. A | 14. A | 19. B |
| 5. B | 10. C | 15. B | 20. A |

# EXAMINATION SECTION
## TEST 1

DIRECTIONS:
   Each question or incomplete statement is followed by several suggested answers or completions.  Select the one that *BEST* answers the
question or completes the statement.  *PRINT THE LETTER OF THE CORRECT
ANSWER IN THE SPACE AT THE RIGHT.*

1. On April 14, 1999, an accountant issued an unqualified          1. ...
   opinion on the financial statements of the Waldo Company
   for the year ended February 28, 1999.  A structural defect in Waldo's recently completed plant first appeared
   in late 1998, but the accountant did not learn of it until
   April 25, 1999.  On May 1, 1999, the accountant learned
   that the defect would cause material losses to the Company.
   The accountant's *PRIMARY* responsibility is
   A. to determine that immediate steps are taken to inform
      all parties who are relying on information contained
      in the statements
   B. to make certain that the company plans to provide for
      the losses in its financial statements for the year
      ended February 28, 1999
   C. to withdraw his unqualified opinion on the financial
      statements for the year ended February 28, 1999, and
      issue a disclaimer of opinion or an appropriately
      qualified opinion
   D. advisory only since the structural defect was not dis-
      closed until after the completion of field work

2. In connection with a public offering of first mortgage          2. ..A.
   bonds by Ronzoni Corp., the bond underwriter has asked
   Ronzoni's accountant to furnish him with a "comfort
   letter" giving as much assurance as possible relative to
   Ronzoni's unaudited financial statements for the three
   months ended March 31, 1999.  The accountant had expressed an unqualified opinion on Ronzoni's financial
   statements for the year ended December 31, 1998; he has
   performed a limited review of Ronzoni's financial statements for the three months ended March 31, 1999.  Nothing
   has come to his attention that would indicate that the
   March 31, 1999 statements are not properly presented.
   Under these circumstances, the accountant's response to
   the underwriter's request should be to
   A. give negative assurance as to the March 31, 1999
      financial statements but disclaim an opinion on
      these statements
   B. inform the underwriters that no comfort letter is
      possible without an audit of the financial state-
      ments for the three months ended March 31, 1999
   C. furnish to the underwriters an opinion that the
      March 31, 1999 statements are fairly presented
      subject to year-end audit adjustments
   D. furnish to the underwriters a piecemeal opinion
      covering financial statements for the three months
      ended March 31, 1999

3. *One* of the generally accepted auditing standards speci-  3. ...
   fies that the auditor
   A. inspect all fixed assets acquired during the year
   B. base his fees upon cost
   C. make a proper study and evaluation of the existing
      internal control
   D. may not solicit clients

4. An auditor's opinion exception arising from a limita-  4. ...
   tion on the scope of his examination should be explained
   in
   A. a footnote to the financial statements
   B. the auditor's report
   C. both a footnote to the financial statements and
      the auditor's report
   D. both the financial statements (immediately after
      the caption of the item or items which could not
      be verified) and the auditor's report

5. An auditor need make no reference in his report to  5. ...
   limitations on the scope of his audit if he
   A. finds it impracticable to confirm receivables but
      satisfies himself by other procedures
   B. does not audit the financial statements of an unau-
      dited subsidiary that represents 75% of the parent's
      total assets
   C. omits confirmation of receivables at the client's
      request but satisfies himself by other procedures
   D. does not observe the opening inventory and is unable
      to satisfy himself by other procedures

6. An auditor's "except for" report is a type of  6. ...
   A. adverse opinion            B. "subject to" opinion
   C. qualified opinion          D. disclaimer of opinion

7. The opinion paragraph of an accountant's report begins:  7. ...
   "In our opinion, based upon our examination and the report of other auditors, the accompanying consolidated
   balance sheet and consolidated statements of income and
   retained earnings and of changes in financial position
   present fairly ...."
   This is a(n)
   A. partial disclaimer of opinion  B. unqualified opinion
   C. "except for" opinion           D. qualified opinion

8. Even though he is expressing an unqualified opinion on  8. ...
   the financial statements of Tigris Corporation, an ac-
   countant feels that readers of the financial statements
   should be aware of an unusual auditing procedure that he
   used.
   For this purpose, he should describe the procedure in the
   A. general representation letter
   B. opinion paragraph of his report
   C. scope paragraph of his report
   D. footnotes to the financial statements

9. Approximately 90% of Rubinstein's Holding Company's  9. ...
   assets consist of investments in wholly owned subsidiary companies.  The accountant examining Rubinstein's financial statements has satisfied himself that
   changes in underlying equity in these investments have

been properly computed based upon the subsidiaries' unaudited financial statements, but he has not examined
the subsidiaries' financial statements.
The auditor's report should include a(n)
   A. adverse opinion          B. "except for" opinion
   C. "subject to" opinion    —D. disclaimer of opinion
10. An accountant has been engaged to prepare unaudited     10. ...
financial statements for his client.
*Which* of the following statements *BEST* describes this
engagement?  The
   A. accountant must perform the basic accepted auditing
      standards necessary to determine that the statements
      are in conformity with generally accepted accounting
      principles
  —B. accountant is performing an accounting service rather
      than an examination of the financial statements
   C. financial statements are representations of both
      management and the accountant
   D. accountant may prepare the statements from the books,
      but may not assist in adjusting and closing the books
11. The accountant's reporting responsibilities are *NOT*    11. ...
met by attaching an explanation of the circumstances
and a disclaimer of opinion to financial statements if
the accountant
   A. has neither confirmed receivables nor observed the
      taking of the physical inventory
   B. believes that the financial statements are false or
      misleading
   C. is uncertain about the outcome of a material contin-
      gency
   D. has not performed sufficient auditing procedures to
      express an opinion
12. Footnotes to financial statements should *NOT* be used to  12. ...
   A. describe the nature and effect of a change in ac-
      counting principles
   B. identify substantial differences between book and
      tax income
   C. correct an improper financial statement presentation
   D. indicate bases for valuing assets
13. Assuming that none of the following has been disclosed  13. ...
in the financial statements, the *MOST* appropriate item
for footnote disclosure is the
   A. collection of all receivables subsequent to year-end
   B. revision of employees' pension plan
   C. retirement of president of company and election of
      new president
   D. material decrease in the advertising budget for the
      coming year and its anticipated effect upon income
14. An exception in the auditor's report because of the lack  14. ...
of consistent application of generally accepted account-
ing principles *MOST* likely would be required in the event
of
   A. a change in the rate of provision for uncollectible
      accounts based upon collection experience
   B. the original adoption of a pension plan for employees

C. inclusion of a previously unconsolidated subsidiary
in consolidated financial statements
D. the revision of pension plan actuarial assumptions
based upon experience

15. An accountant who believes the occurrence rate of a          15. ...
certain characteristic in a population being examined
is 3% and who has established a maximum acceptable occurrence rate at 5%, should use a(n) _____ sampling plan.
   A. attribute  B. discovery  C. stratified D. variable

16. For good internal control, the monthly bank statements       16. ...
should be reconciled by someone under the direction of the
   A. credit manager          B. controller
   C. cashier                 D. treasurer

17. For good internal control, the person who should sign        17. ...
checks is the
   A. person preparing the checks  B. purchasing agent
   C. accounts-payable clerk        D. treasurer

18. For good internal control, the credit manager should be      18. ...
responsible to the
   A. sales manager           B. customer-service manager
   C. controller              D. treasurer

19. For good internal control, the billing department should     19. ...
be under the direction of the
   A. controller              B. credit manager
   C. sales manager           D. treasurer

20. The authorization for write-off of accounts receivable       20. ...
should be the responsibility of the
   A. credit manager          B. controller
   C. accounts-receivable clerk  D. treasurer

————

# KEY (CORRECT ANSWERS)

| | | | |
|---|---|---|---|
| 1. | A | 11. | B |
| 2. | A | 12. | C |
| 3. | C | 13. | B |
| 4. | B | 14. | C |
| 5. | A | 15. | A |
| 6. | C | 16. | B |
| 7. | B | 17. | D |
| 8. | C | 18. | D |
| 9. | D | 19. | A |
| 10. | B | 20. | D |

————

# TEST 2

DIRECTIONS:
Each question or incomplete statement is followed by several suggested answers or completions. Select the one that *BEST* answers the
question or completes the statement. *PRINT THE LETTER OF THE CORRECT
ANSWER IN THE SPACE AT THE RIGHT.*

1. Emerson, Inc., has a June 30 year-end. Its bank mails        1. ...
   bank statements each Friday of every week and on the
   last business day of each month.
   For year-end, Saturday, June 30, 1999, the auditor should
   have the client ask the bank to mail directly to the auditor
   A. *only* the June 29 bank statement
   B. *only* the July 13 bank statement
   C. *both* the June 29 and July 6 bank statements
   D. *both* the July 6 and 13 bank statements
2. Uranus Company has a separate outside transfer agent and      2. ...
   outside registrar for its common stock.
   A confirmation request sent to the transfer agent should
   ask for
   A. a list of all stockholders and the number of shares
      issued to each
   B. a statement from the agent that all surrendered
      certificates have been effectively canceled
   C. total shares issued, shares issued in name of client,
      and unbilled fees
   D. total shares authorized
3. The Miller Company records checks as being issued on the      3. ...
   day they are written; however, the checks are often held
   a number of days before being released.
   The audit procedure which is *LEAST* likely to reveal this
   method of incorrect cash-disbursements cutoff is to
   A. examine checks returned with cutoff bank statement
      for unreasonable time lag between date recorded in
      cash-disbursements book and date clearing bank
   B. reconcile vendors' invoices with accounts payable
      per books
   C. reconcile bank statement at year-end
   D. reconcile exceptions to account-payable confirmations
4. The Sandman Corporation uses prenumbered receiving re-        4. ...
   ports which are released in numerical order from a locked
   box. For two days before the physical count, all receiving
   reports are stamped "before inventory," and, for two days
   after the physical count, all receiving reports are stamped
   "after inventory." The receiving department continues to
   receive goods after the cutoff time while the physical
   count is in process.
   The *LEAST* efficient method for checking the accuracy of
   the cutoff is to
   A. list the number of the last receiving report for
      items included in the physical-inventory count
   B. observe that the receiving clerk is stamping the
      receiving reports properly

5

    C. test trace receiving reports issued before the last receiving report to the physical items to see that they have been included in the physical count

    D. test trace receiving reports issued after the last receiving report to the physical items to see that they have not been included in the physical count

5. Lustig & Co., accountants, are the auditors of Ledley     5. ...
Corporation which has a subsidiary audited by Tompkins
& Co., accountants. Tompkins issued a qualified opinion
on the financial statements of the subsidiary because of
an uncertainly on the recovery of deferred-research-and-
development costs.
Lustig can issue an unqualified opinion on the consolidated financial statements of Leslie and subsidiaries
*only if*

    A. the amount of the subsidiary's deferred-research-and-development costs is not material in relation to the consolidated statements

    B. Lustig is able to satisfy itself as to the independence and professional reputation of Tompkins

    C. Lustig is able to satisfy itself as to the independence and professional reputation of Tompkins and also take appropriate steps to satisfy itself as to the quality of Tompkin's examination

    D. Lustig makes reference in its report to the examination of the subsidiary by Tompkins

6. Benn, Inc., carries its investment in Monania Corpora-     6. ...
tion at equity. Benn's investment in Monania accounts
for 45% of the total assets of Benn. Benn and Monania
are not audited by the same accountant.
In order for Benn's auditor to issue an unqualified
opinion in regard to the value of Benn's investment in
Monania and the income derived therefrom, Benn's auditor

    A. needs to obtain only Monania's unaudited financial statements

    B. needs to obtain only Monania's audited financial statements

    C. must obtain Monania's audited financial statements and make inquiries concerning the professional reputation and independence of Monania's auditor

    D. must review the working papers of Monania's auditor

7. Devore, Inc., which has a December 31 year-end, closed     7. ...
an out-of-town division on April 21, 1998. The checking
account used by the division at a local bank was closed
out as of April 21, 1998. The bank, however, has continued to mail bank statements, with zero balances, as
of the fifth of each month. Devore has requested the
bank to mail the January 5, 1999 bank statement directly
to its independent auditor.
For this closed checking account during his examination
for 1998, the auditor should *ordinarily*

    A. review *only* the January 5, 1999, bank statement

    B. review *only* the bank statement for 1998

    C. review *only* the bank statements for 1998 and the January 5, 1999, statement

    D. send a bank confirmation as of December 31, 1998, in addition to reviewing the bank statements for 1998 and the January 5, 1999, statement

8. The audit step *MOST* likely to reveal the existence of contingent liabilities is:
    A. A review of vouchers paid during the month following the year-end
    B. Account-payable confirmations
    C. An inquiry directed to legal counsel
    D. Mortgage-note confirmation

    8. ...

9. *One* of the *MAJOR* audit procedures for determining whether the allowance for doubtful receivables is adequate is
    A. the preparation of a list of aged accounts receivable
    B. confirming any account receivable written off during the year
    C. vouching the collection on any account receivable written off in prior periods
    D. confirming any account receivable with a credit balance

    9. ...

10. One of the *better* ways for an auditor to detect kiting is to
    A. request a cut-off bank statement
    B. send a bank confirmation
    C. prepare a bank-transfer working paper
    D. prepare a bank reconciliation at year-end

    10. ...

11. A company uses the account code 448 for maintenance expense. However, one of the company's clerks often codes maintenance expense as 844. The highest account code in the system is 800.
*What* would be the *BEST* internal control check to build into the company's computer program to detect this error?
    A. A check for this type of error would have to be made before the information was transmitted to the EDP department
    B. Valid-character test    C. Sequence check
    D. Valid-code test

    11. ...

12. Parsons is the executive partner of Parsons & Co., accountants. One of its smaller clients is a large non-profit charitable organization. The organization has asked Parsons to be on its board of directors which consists of a large number of the community's leaders. Membership on the board is honorary in nature.
Parsons & Co. would be considered to be independent
    A. under *no* circumstances
    B. as long as Parsons' directorship was disclosed in the organization's financial statements
    C. as long as Parsons was *not* directly in charge of the audit
    D. as long as Parsons does *not* perform or give advice on management functions of the organization

    12. ...

13. Godley, a non-CPA, has a law practice. Godley has recommended one of his clients to Dawson, CPA. Dawson has agreed to pay Godley 10% of the fee for services rendered by Dawson to Godley's client.

    13. ...

Who, if anyone, is in violation of the Code of Professional Ethics?
    A. *Both* Godley and Dawson    B. *Neither* Godley nor Dawson
    C. *Only* Godette    D. *Only* Dawson

14. The general group of the generally accepted auditing   14. ...
standards includes a requirement that
    A. the field work be adequately planned and supervised
    B. the auditor's report state whether or not the financial statements conform to generally accepted accounting principles
    C. due professional care be exercised by the auditor
    D. informative disclosures in the financial statements be reasonably adequate

15. Approximately 95% of returned positive account-receivable   15. ...
confirmations indicated that the customer owed a smaller balance than the amount confirmed.
This might be explained by the fact that
    A. the cash-receipts journal was held open after year-end
    B. there is a large number of unrecorded liabilities
    C. the sales journal was closed prior to year-end
    D. the sales journal was held open after year-end

16. An auditor should examine minutes of board of directors'   16. ...
meetings
    A. through the date of his report
    B. through the date of the financial statements
    C. on a test basis
    D. only at the beginning of the audit

17. The return of a positive account-receivable confirma-   17. ...
tion without an exception attests to the
    A. collectibility of the receivable balance
    B. accuracy of the receivable balance
    C. accuracy of the aging of accounts receivable
    D. accuracy of the allowance for bad debts

18. During his examination of a January 19, 1999, **cut-off**   18. ...
bank statement, an auditor noticed that the majority of checks listed as outstanding at December 31, 1998 **had** not cleared the bank. This would indicate:
    A. A high probability of lapping
    B. A high probability of kiting
    C. That the cash-disbursements journal had been held open past December 31, 1998
    D. That the cash-disbursements journal had been closed prior to December 31, 1998

19. A *PRINCIPAL* purpose of a letter of representation from   19. ...
management is to
    A. serve as an introduction to company personnel and an authorization to examine the records
    B. discharge the auditor from legal liability for his examination
    C. confirm in writing management's approval of limitations on the scope of the audit
    D. remind management of its primary responsibility for financial statements

20. As the specified reliability is increased in a discovery   20. ...
    sampling plan for any given population and maximum oc-
    currence rate, the required sample size
    A. increases                    B. decreases
    C. remains the same             D. cannot be determined

_____

# KEY (CORRECT ANSWERS)

|      |   |      |   |
|------|---|------|---|
| 1.   | D | 11.  | D |
| 2.   | C | 12.  | D |
| 3.   | C | 13.  | D |
| 4.   | B | 14.  | C |
| 5.   | A | 15.  | D |
| 6.   | C | 16.  | A |
| 7.   | D | 17.  | B |
| 8.   | C | 18.  | C |
| 9.   | A | 19.  | D |
| 10.  | C | 20.  | A |

_____

# EXAMINATION SECTION
## TEST 1

DIRECTIONS: Each question or incomplete statement is followed by several suggested answers or completions. Select the one that BEST answers the question or completes the statement. *PRINT THE LETTER OF THE CORRECT ANSWER IN THE SPACE AT THE RIGHT.*

1. Which of the following is NOT usually performed by the accountant in a review engagement of a nonpublic entity?   1.\_\_\_\_

    A. Writing an engagement letter to establish an understanding regarding the services to be performed.
    B. Issuing a report stating that the review was performed in accordance with standards established by the AICPA.
    C. Communicating any material weaknesses discovered during the study and evaluation of internal accounting control.
    D. Reading the financial statements to consider whether they conform with generally accepted accounting principles.

2. When the financial statements are prepared on the going concern basis but the auditor concludes there is substantial doubt whether the client can continue in existence and also believes there are uncertainties about the recoverability of recorded asset amounts on the financial statements, the auditor may issue a(n)   2.\_\_\_\_

    A. adverse opinion
    B. *except for* qualified opinion
    C. *subject to* qualified opinion
    D. unqualified opinion with an explanatory separate paragraph

3. A small client recently put its cash disbursements system on a microcomputer. About which of the following internal accounting control features would an auditor MOST likely be concerned?   3.\_\_\_\_

    A. Programming of this microcomputer is in BASIC, although COBOL is the dominant, standard language for business processing.
    B. This microcomputer is operated by employees who have other, non-data-processing job responsibilities.
    C. The microcomputer terminal is physically close to the computer and directly connected to it.
    D. There are restrictions on the amount of data that can be stored and on the length of time that data can be stored.

4. When an independent accountant issues a comfort letter to an underwriter containing comments on data that have not been audited, the underwriter MOST likely will receive   4.\_\_\_\_

    A. a disclaimer on prospective financial statements
    B. a limited opinion on *pro forma* financial statements
    C. positive assurance on supplementary disclosures
    D. negative assurance on capsule information

5. When an auditor conducts an examination in accordance with generally accepted auditing standards and concludes that the financial statements are fairly presented in accordance with a comprehensive basis of accounting other than generally accepted accounting principles such as the cash basis of accounting, the auditor should issue a

    A.  disclaimer of opinion         B.  review report
    C.  qualified opinion            D.  special report

6. A limitation on the scope of the auditor's examination sufficient to preclude an unqualified opinion will ALWAYS result when management

    A.  asks the auditor to report on the balance sheet and not on the other basic financial statements
    B.  refuses to permit its lawyer to respond to the letter of audit inquiry
    C.  discloses material related party transactions in the footnotes to the financial statements
    D.  knows that confirmation of accounts receivable is not feasible

7. Which of the following audit procedures would an auditor be LEAST likely to perform using a generalized computer audit program?

    A.  Searching records of accounts receivable balances for credit balances
    B.  Investigating inventory balances for possible obsolescence
    C.  Selecting accounts receivable for positive and negative confirmation
    D.  Listing of unusually large inventory balances

8. An auditor evaluates the existing system of internal accounting control PRIMARILY to

    A.  ascertain whether employees adhere to managerial policies
    B.  determine the extent of substantive tests that must be performed
    C.  determine whether procedures and records concerning the safeguarding of assets are reliable
    D.  establish a basis for deciding which compliance tests are necessary

9. When an independent CPA is associated with the financial statements of a publicly held entity but has not audited or reviewed such statements, the appropriate form of report to be issued must include a(n)

    A.  disclaimer of opinion
    B.  compilation report
    C.  adverse opinion
    D.  unaudited association report

10. An auditor includes a separate paragraph in an otherwise unqualified report to emphasize that the entity being reported upon had significant transactions with related parties. The inclusion of this separate paragraph

    A.  violates generally accepted auditing standards if this information is already disclosed in footnotes to the financial statements
    B.  necessitates a revision of the opinion paragraph to include the phrase *with the foregoing explanation*
    C.  is appropriate and would not negate the unqualified opinion
    D.  is considered an *except for* qualification of the report

11. Which of the following requires recognition in the auditor's opinion as to consistency?   11.____

    A. The correction of an error in the prior year's financial statements resulting from a mathematical mistake in capitalizing interest
    B. The change from the cost method to the equity method of accounting for investments in common stock
    C. A change in the estimate of provisions for warranty costs
    D. A change in depreciation method which has no effect on current year's financial statements but is certain to affect future years

12. The auditor who intends to express a qualified opinion should disclose all the substantive reasons in a separate explanatory paragraph of the report EXCEPT when the opinion paragraph   12.____

    A. makes reference to a contingent liability
    B. describes a limitation on the scope of the examination
    C. describes the use of an accounting principle at variance with generally accepted accounting principles
    D. makes reference to a change in accounting principle

13. When an examination is made in accordance with generally accepted auditing standards, the auditor should ALWAYS   13.____

    A. document the auditor's understanding of the client's internal accounting control system
    B. employ analytical review procedures
    C. obtain certain written representations from management
    D. observe the taking of physical inventory on the balance sheet date

14. Which of the following flowchart symbols represents online storage?   14.____

    A.

    B.

    C.

    D.

15. What is the continuing auditor's obligation concerning the discovery at an interim date of a material weakness in the internal accounting control of a client if this same weakness had been communicated to the client during the prior year's audit?
The auditor   15.____

    A. should communicate this weakness to the client immediately because the discovery of such weaknesses in internal accounting control is the purpose of a review of interim financial information
    B. need not communicate this weakness to the client because it had already been communicated the prior year

C. should communicate this weakness to the client following completion of the examination unless the auditor decides to communicate it to the client at the interim date

D. should extend the audit procedures to investigate whether this weakness had any effect on the prior year's financial statements

16. To achieve good internal accounting control, which department should perform the activities of matching shipping documents with sales orders and preparing daily sales summaries?

    A. Billing                      B. Shipping
    C. Credit                      D. Sales order

17. A PRIMARY advantage of using generalized audit software packages in auditing the financial statements of a client that uses an EDP system is that the auditor may

A. substantiate the accuracy of data through self-checking digits and hash totals

B. access information stored on computer files without a complete understanding of the client's hardware and software features

C. reduce the level of required compliance testing to a relatively small amount

D. gather and permanently store large quantities of supportive evidential matter in machine readable form

18. An auditor is concerned with completing various phases of the examination after the balance sheet date.
This subsequent period extends to the date of the

A. auditor's report

B. final review of the audit working papers

C. public issuance of the financial statements

D. delivery of the auditor's report to the client

19. The permanent file section of the working papers that is kept for each audit client MOST likely contains

A. review notes pertaining to questions and comments regarding the audit work performed

B. a schedule of time spent on the engagement by each individual auditor

C. correspondence with the client's legal counsel concerning pending litigation

D. narrative descriptions of the client's accounting procedures and internal accounting controls

20. If, after completing the review of the design of internal accounting controls, the auditor plans to rely on internal accounting control procedures pertaining to plant asset transactions, the auditor should NEXT

A. make extensive substantive tests of plant asset balances

B. establish the physical existence of current year additions

C. complete the plant asset section of the internal accounting control questionnaire

D. perform compliance tests of the controls expected to be relied upon

21. Sound internal accounting control procedures dictate that defective merchandise returned by customers should be presented to the _____ clerk.

    A. purchasing                B. receiving
    C. inventory control       D. sales

21.____

22. In a properly designed accounts payable system, a voucher is prepared after the invoice, purchase order, requisition, and receiving report are verified.
The NEXT step in the system is to

    A. cancel the supporting documents
    B. enter the check amount in the check register
    C. approve the voucher for payment
    D. post the voucher amount to the expense ledger

22.____

23. Alpha Company uses its sales invoices for posting perpetual inventory records. Inadequate internal accounting controls over the invoicing function allow goods to be shipped that are not invoiced.
The inadequate controls could cause an

    A. understatement of revenues, receivables, and inventory
    B. overstatement of revenues and receivables, and an understatement of inventory
    C. understatement of revenues and receivables, and an overstatement of inventory
    D. overstatement of revenues, receivables, and inventory

23.____

24. After an auditor had been engaged to perform the first audit for a nonpublic entity, the client requested to change the engagement to a review.
In which of the following situations would there be a reasonable basis to comply with the client's request?

    A. The client's bank required an audit before committing to a loan, but the client subsequently acquired alternative financing.
    B. The auditor was prohibited by the client from corresponding with the client's legal counsel.
    C. Management refused to sign the client representation letter.
    D. The auditing procedures were substantially complete and the auditor determined that an unqualified opinion was warranted, but there was a disagreement concerning the audit fee.

24.____

25. Which of the following statements BEST describe the auditor's responsibility regarding the detection of material irregularities?

    A. Because of the inherent limitations of an audit, the auditor is not responsible for the failure to detect material irregularities.
    B. The auditor is responsible for the failure to detect material irregularities when such failure results from nonperformance of audit procedures specifically described in the engagement letter.
    C. The auditor should extend auditing procedures to actively search for evidence of material irregularities where the examination indicates that material irregularities may exist.
    D. The auditor is responsible for the failure to detect material irregularities when the auditor's evaluation of internal accounting control indicates that there is no basis for any reliance thereon.

25.____

26. Comparative financial statements include the financial statements of a prior period which were examined by a predecessor auditor whose report is not presented.
If the predecessor auditor's report was qualified, the successor auditor MUST

    A. obtain written approval from the predecessor auditor to include the prior year's financial statements
    B. issue a standard comparative audit report indicating the division of responsibility
    C. express an opinion on the current year statements alone and make no reference to the prior year statements
    D. disclose the reasons for any qualification in the predecessor auditor's opinion

26._

27. The auditor may conclude that depreciation charges are insufficient by noting

    A. large amounts of fully depreciated assets
    B. continuous trade-ins of relatively new assets
    C. excessive recurring losses on assets retired
    D. insured values greatly in excess of book values

27._

28. An auditor compares yearly revenues and expenses with those of the prior year and investigates all changes exceeding 10%.
By this procedure, the auditor would be MOST likely to learn that

    A. fourth quarter payroll taxes were not paid
    B. the client changed its capitalization policy for small tools for the year
    C. an increase in property tax rates has not been recognized in the client's accrual
    D. the yearly provision for uncollectible accounts is inadequate because of worsening economic conditions

28._

29. The development of constructive suggestions to clients for improvements in internal accounting control is

    A. a requirement of the auditor's study and evaluation of internal accounting control
    B. a desirable by-product of an audit engagement
    C. addressed by the auditor only during a special engagement
    D. as important as establishing a basis for reliance upon the internal accounting control system

29._

30. Of the following statements about an internal accounting control system, which one is CORRECT?

    A. The maintenance of the system of internal accounting control is an important responsibility of the internal auditor.
    B. Administrative controls relate directly to the safeguarding of assets and the systems of authorization and approval.
    C. Because of the cost/benefit relationship, internal accounting control procedures may be applied on a test basis in some circumstances.
    D. Internal accounting control procedures reasonably ensure that collusion among employees cannot occur.

30._

# KEY (CORRECT ANSWERS)

| | | | | |
|---|---|---|---|---|
| 1. | C | | 16. | A |
| 2. | C | | 17. | B |
| 3. | B | | 18. | A |
| 4. | D | | 19. | D |
| 5. | D | | 20. | D |
| | | | | |
| 6. | B | | 21. | B |
| 7. | B | | 22. | C |
| 8. | B | | 23. | C |
| 9. | A | | 24. | A |
| 10. | C | | 25. | C |
| | | | | |
| 11. | B | | 26. | D |
| 12. | D | | 27. | C |
| 13. | C | | 28. | B |
| 14. | A | | 29. | B |
| 15. | C | | 30. | C |

———

# TEST 2

DIRECTIONS: Each question or incomplete statement is followed by several suggested answers or completions. Select the one that BEST answers the question or completes the statement. *PRINT THE LETTER OF THE CORRECT ANSWER IN THE SPACE AT THE RIGHT.*

1. Which of the following statistical sampling methods is MOST useful to auditors when testing for compliance?    1.___

   A. Ratio estimation
   C. Difference estimation
   B. Variable sampling
   D. Discovery sampling

2. If after completing the preliminary phase of the review of the internal accounting control system the auditor plans to rely on the system, the auditor should NEXT    2.___

   A. trace several transactions through the related documents and records to observe the related internal accounting control procedures in operation
   B. perform compliance tests to provide reasonable assurance that the accounting control procedures are being applied as prescribed
   C. complete the review of the system to determine whether the accounting control procedures are suitably designed
   D. design substantive tests that contemplate reliance on the system of internal accounting control

3. The form of communication with a client in a management advisory service consultation should be    3.___

   A. either oral or written
   B. oral with appropriate documentation in the workpapers
   C. written and copies should be sent to both management and the board of directors
   D. written and a copy should be sent to management alone

4. Which of the following control procedures may prevent the failure to bill customers for some shipments?    4.___

   A. Each shipment should be supported by a prenumbered sales invoice that is accounted for.
   B. Each sales order should be approved by authorized personnel.
   C. Sales journal entries should be reconciled to daily sales summaries.
   D. Each sales invoice should be supported by a shipping document.

5. A part of the auditor's planning of an audit engagement should be a plan to search for    5.___

   A. errors or irregularities that would have a material or immaterial effect on the financial statements
   B. errors or irregularities that would have a material effect on the financial statements
   C. errors that would have a material effect on the financial statements, but the auditor need not plan to search for irregularities
   D. irregularities that would have a material effect on the financial statements, but the auditor need not plan to search for errors

6. In a study and evaluation of the system of internal accounting control, the completion of a questionnaire is MOST closely associated with which of the following?　　6._____

    A. Tests of compliance
    B. Substantive tests
    C. Preliminary evaluation of the system
    D. Review of the system design

7. The audit work performed by each assistant should be reviewed to determine whether it was adequately performed and to evaluate whether　　7._____

    A. there has been a thorough documentation of the internal accounting controls
    B. the auditor's system of quality control has been maintained at a high level
    C. the assistants' preliminary judgments about materiality differ from the materiality levels of the persons who will rely on the financial statements
    D. the results are consistent with the conclusions to be presented in the auditor's report

8. During a review of the financial statements of a nonpublic entity, the CPA finds that the financial statements contain a material departure from generally accepted accounting principles.
If management refuses to correct the financial statement presentations, the CPA should　　8._____

    A. attach a footnote explaining the effects of the departure
    B. disclose the departure in a separate paragraph of the report
    C. issue a compilation report
    D. issue an adverse opinion

9. The profession's ethical standards would MOST likely be considered to have been violated when the CPA represents that specific consulting services will be performed for a stated fee and it is apparent at the time of the representation that the　　9._____

    A. CPA would not be independent
    B. fee was a competitive bid
    C. actual fee would be substantially higher
    D. actual fee would be substantially lower than the fees charged by other CPAs for comparable services

10. After the preliminary phase of the review of a client's EDP controls, an auditor may decide not to perform compliance tests related to the control procedures within the EDP portion of the client's internal accounting control system.
Which of the following would NOT be a valid reason for choosing to omit compliance tests?　　10._____

    A. The controls appear adequate.
    B. The controls duplicate operative controls existing elsewhere in the system.
    C. There appear to be major weaknesses that would preclude reliance on the stated procedure.
    D. The time and dollar costs of testing exceed the time and dollar savings in substantive testing if the compliance tests show the controls to be operative.

11. Before applying principal substantive tests to the details of asset and liability accounts at     11.___
an interim date, the auditor should

   A. assess the difficulty in controlling incremental audit risk
   B. investigate significant fluctuations that have occurred in the asset and liability accounts since the previous balance sheet date
   C. select only those accounts which can effectively be sampled during year-end audit work
   D. consider the compliance tests that must be applied at the balance sheet date to extend the audit conclusions reached at the interim date

12. A violation of the profession's ethical standards would MOST likely occur when a CPA     12.___
who

   A. is also admitted to the Bar represents on letterhead to be both an attorney and a CPA
   B. writes a newsletter on financial management also permits a publishing company to solicit subscriptions by direct mail
   C. is controller of a bank permits the bank to use the controller's CPA title in the listing of officers in its publications
   D. is the sole shareholder in a professional accountancy corporation that uses the designation *and company* in the firm title

13. After beginning an audit of a new client, Larkin, CPA, discovers that the professional     13.___
competence necessary for the engagement is lacking. Larkin informs management of the situation and recommends another CPA, and management engages the other CPA. Under these circumstances,

   A. Larkin's lack of competence should be construed to be a violation of generally accepted auditing standards
   B. Larkin may request compensation from the client for any professional services rendered to it in connection with the audit
   C. Larkin's request for a commission from the other CPA is permitted because a more competent audit can now be performed
   D. Larkin may be indebted to the other CPA since the other CPA can collect from the client only the amount the client originally agreed to pay Larkin

14. Which of the following BEST describes what is meant by generally accepted auditing     14.___
standards?

   A. Pronouncements issued by the Auditing Standards Board
   B. Procedures to be used to gather evidence to support financial statements
   C. Rules acknowledged by the accounting profession because of their universal compliance
   D. Measures of the quality of the auditor's performance

15. A CPA purchased stock in a client corporation and placed it in a trust as an educational     15.___
fund for the CPA's minor child. The trust securities were not material to the CPA but were material to the child's personal net worth. Would the independence of the CPA be considered to be impaired with respect to the client?

   A. *Yes,* because the stock would be considered a direct financial interest and, consequently, materiality is not a factor

B. *Yes,* because the stock would be considered an indirect financial interest that is material to the CPA's child

C. *No,* because the CPA would not be considered to have a direct financial interest in the client

D. *No,* because the CPA would not be considered to have a material indirect financial interest in the client

16. The auditor concludes that there is a material inconsistency in the other information in an annual report to shareholders containing audited financial statements.
If the client refuses to revise or eliminate the material inconsistency, the auditor should

16.\_\_\_\_

A. revise the auditor's report to include a separate explanatory paragraph describing the material inconsistency
B. consult with a party whose advice might influence the client, such as the client's legal counsel
C. issue a qualified opinion after discussing the matter with the client's board of directors
D. consider the matter closed since the other information is not in the audited financial statements

17. One of the major problems in an EDP system is that incompatible functions may be performed by the same individual. One compensating control for this is the use of

17.\_\_\_\_

A. a self-checking digit system
B. echo checks
C. a computer log
D. computer-generated hash totals

18. An auditor plans to examine a sample of 20 purchase orders for proper approvals as prescribed by the client's internal accounting control procedures. One of the purchase orders in the chosen sample of 20 cannot be found, and the auditor is unable to use alternative procedures to test whether that purchase order was properly approved. The auditor should

18.\_\_\_\_

A. choose another purchase order to replace the missing purchase order in the sample
B. consider this compliance test invalid and proceed with substantive tests since internal accounting control cannot be relied upon
C. treat the missing purchase order as a deviation for the purpose of evaluating the sample
D. select a completely new set of 20 purchase orders

19. Where computer processing is used in significant accounting applications, internal accounting control procedures may be defined by classifying control procedures into two types: general and

19.\_\_\_\_

A. administrative
C. application
B. specific
D. authorization

20. The principal auditor is satisfied with the independence and professional reputation of the other auditor who has audited a subsidiary.
To indicate the division of responsibility, the principal auditor should modify

20._

    A. both the scope and opinion paragraphs of the report
    B. only the scope paragraph of the report
    C. only the opinion paragraph of the report
    D. only the opinion paragraph of the report and include an explanatory middle paragraph

21. When the auditor is unable to determine the amounts associated with the illegal acts of client personnel because of an inability to obtain adequate evidence, the auditor should issue a(n)

21._

    A. *subject to* qualified opinion
    B. disclaimer of opinion
    C. adverse opinion
    D. unqualified opinion with a separate explanatory paragraph

22. An auditor would be MOST likely to consider expressing a qualified opinion if the client's financial statements include a footnote on related party transactions that

22._

    A. lists the amounts due from related parties including the terms and manner of settlement
    B. discloses compensating balance arrangements maintained for the benefit of related parties
    C. represents that certain transactions with related parties were consummated on terms equally as favorable as would have been obtained in transactions with unrelated parties
    D. presents the dollar volume of related party transactions and the effects of any change in the method of establishing terms from that of the prior period

23. After issuance of the auditor's report, the auditor has no obligation to make any further inquiries with respect to audited financial statements covered by that report unless

23._

    A. a final resolution of a contingency that had resulted in a qualification of the auditor's report is made
    B. a development occurs that may affect the client's ability to continue as a going concern
    C. an investigation of the auditor's practice by a peer review committee ensues
    D. new information is discovered concerning undisclosed related party transactions of the previously audited period

24. The accountant's report expressing an opinion on an entity's system of internal accounting control would NOT include a

24._

    A. brief explanation of the broad objectives and inherent limitations of internal accounting control
    B. specific date that the report covers, rather than a period of time
    C. statement that the entity's system of internal accounting control is consistent with that of the prior year after giving effect to subsequent changes
    D. description of the scope of the engagement

25. Which of the following legal situations would be considered to impair the auditor's independence?  25.____

    A. An expressed intention by the present management to commence litigation against the auditor alleging deficiencies in audit work for the client, although the auditor considers that there is only a remote possibility that such a claim will be filed

    B. Actual litigation by the auditor against the client for an amount not material to the auditor or to the financial statements of the client arising out of disputes as to billings for management advisory services

    C. Actual litigation by the auditor against the present management alleging management fraud or deceit

    D. Actual litigation by the client against the auditor for an amount not material to the auditor or to the financial statements of the client arising out of disputes as to billings for tax services

26. The PRIMARY reason an auditor requests letters of inquiry be sent to a client's attorneys is to provide the auditor with  26.____

    A. a description and evaluation of litigation, claims, and assessments that existed at the date of the balance sheet

    B. an expert opinion as to whether a loss is possible, probable, or remote

    C. the opportunity to examine the documentation concerning litigation, claims, and assessments

    D. corroboration of the information furnished by management concerning litigation, claims, and assessments

27. In connection with the element of professional development, a CPA firm's system of quality control should ordinarily provide that all personnel  27.____

    A. have the knowledge required to enable them to fulfill responsibilities assigned

    B. possess judgment, motivation, and adequate experience

    C. seek assistance from persons having appropriate levels of knowledge, judgment, and authority

    D. demonstrate compliance with peer review directives

28. Edwards Corp. uses the last-in, first-out method of costing for half of its inventory and the first-in, first-out method of costing for the other half of its inventory.  28.____
Because of these recording and reporting methods, the auditor should issue a(n) _____ opinion.

    A. unqualified               B. disclaimer of

    C. *except for* qualified      D. *subject to* qualified

29. Purchase cutoff procedures should be designed to test whether or not all inventory  29.____

    A. purchased and received before the end of the year was paid for

    B. ordered before the end of the year was received

    C. purchased and received before the end of the year was recorded

    D. owned by the company is in the possession of the company at the end of the year

30. Matthews Corp. has changed from a system of recording time worked on clock cards to a     30._
computerized payroll system in which employees record time in and out with magnetic
cards. The EDP system automatically updates all payroll records.
Because of this change,

   A.   a generalized computer audit program must be used
   B.   part of the audit trail is altered
   C.   the potential for payroll related fraud is diminished
   D.   transactions must be processed in batches

_____

# KEY (CORRECT ANSWERS)

|     |   |     |   |
|-----|---|-----|---|
| 1.  | D | 16. | A |
| 2.  | C | 17. | C |
| 3.  | A | 18. | C |
| 4.  | A | 19. | C |
| 5.  | B | 20. | A |
| 6.  | D | 21. | B |
| 7.  | D | 22. | C |
| 8.  | B | 23. | D |
| 9.  | C | 24. | C |
| 10. | A | 25. | C |
| 11. | A | 26. | D |
| 12. | D | 27. | A |
| 13. | B | 28. | A |
| 14. | D | 29. | C |
| 15. | A | 30. | B |

_____

# EXAMINATION SECTION

# TEST 1

DIRECTIONS: Each question or incomplete statement is followed by several suggested answers or completions. Select the one that BEST answers the question or completes the statement. *PRINT THE LETTER OF THE CORRECT ANSWER IN THE SPACE AT THE RIGHT.*

1. Comfort letters are ordinarily signed by the       1.___
   A. client
   C. independent auditor
   B. client's lawyer
   D. internal auditor

2. If a publicly held entity declines to include in its       2.___
   financial report supplementary information required by
   the FASB, the auditor should issue
   A. an unqualified opinion with a separate explanatory
      paragraph
   B. either a disclaimer of opinion or an adverse opinion
   C. either an *except for* qualified opinion or a disclaimer
      of opinion
   D. either an adverse opinion or an *except for* qualified
      opinion

3. An auditor's report would be designated as a special       3.___
   report when it is issued in connection with financial
   statements that are
   A. for an interim period and are subjected to a limited
      review
   B. unaudited and are prepared from a client's accounting
      records
   C. prepared in accordance with a comprehensive basis of
      accounting other than generally accepted accounting
      principles
   D. purported to be in accordance with generally accepted
      accounting principles but do not include a presenta-
      tion of the statement of changes in financial
      position

4. The objective of a review of interim financial information   4.___
   is to provide the accountant with a basis for reporting
   whether
   A. a reasonable basis exists for expressing an updated
      opinion regarding the financial statements that were
      previously audited
   B. material modifications should be made to conform with
      generally accepted accounting principles
   C. the financial statements are presented fairly in
      accordance with standards of interim reporting
   D. the financial statements are presented fairly in
      accordance with generally accepted accounting prin-
      ciples

5. In which of the following circumstances would an auditor    5.___
   be MOST likely to express an adverse opinion?
   A. The statements are not in conformity with the FASB
      statements regarding the capitalization of leases.
   B. Information comes to the auditor's attention that
      raises substantial doubt about the entity's ability
      to continue in existence.
   C. The chief executive officer refuses the auditor access
      to minutes of board of directors' meetings.
   D. Compliance tests show that the entity's system of
      internal accounting control is so poor that it cannot
      be relied upon

6. When an auditor reissues in 1993 the auditor's report on    6.___
   the 1990 financial statements at the request of the
   client without revising the 1990 wording, the auditor
   should
   A. use the date of the original report
   B. use the date of the client's request
   C. use the date of the current period report
   D. dual date the report

7. When reporting on comparative financial statements, which   7.___
   of the following circumstances ordinarily should cause
   the auditor to change the previously issued opinion on
   the prior year's financial statements?
   A. A change in accounting principle caused a consistency
      exception in the current year's auditor's report.
   B. The prior year opinion was unqualified and the
      current year opinion was qualified due to a scope
      limitation.
   C. A major uncertainty that caused a qualified opinion
      on the prior year's financial statements was resolved
      during the current year.
   D. None of the above

8. When reporting on comparative financial statements where    8.___
   the financial statements of the prior year have been
   examined by a predecessor auditor whose report is not
   presented, the successor auditor should make
   A. no reference to the predecessor auditor
   B. reference to the predecessor auditor only if the
      predecessor auditor expressed a qualified opinion
   C. reference to the predecessor auditor only if the
      predecessor auditor expressed an unqualified opinion
   D. reference to the predecessor auditor regardless of
      the type of opinion expressed by the predecessor
      auditor

9. If an accountant concludes that unaudited financial state-  9.___
   ments on which the accountant is disclaiming an opinion
   also lack adequate disclosure, the accountant should
   suggest appropriate revision.
   If the client does NOT accept the accountant's suggestion,
   the accountant should

    A. issue an adverse opinion and describe the appropriate revision in the report

    B. make reference to the appropriate revision and issue a modified report expressing limited assurance

    C. describe the appropriate revision to the financial statements in the accountant's disclaimer of opinion

    D. accept the client's inaction because the statements are unaudited and the accountant has disclaimed an opinion

10. Under which of the following circumstances would a dis-    10.___
claimer of opinion NOT be appropriate? The

    A. financial statements fail to contain adequate disclosure concerning related party transactions

    B. client refuses to permit its attorney to furnish information requested in a letter of audit inquiry

    C. auditor is engaged after fiscal year-end and is unable to observe physical inventories or apply alternative procedures to verify their balances

    D. auditor is unable to determine the amounts associated with illegal acts committed by the client's management

11. Which of the following should NOT be included in an    11.___
accountant's standard report based upon the compilation of an entity's financial statements? A statement that

    A. a compilation is limited to presenting in the form of financial statements information that is the representation of management

    B. the compilation was performed in accordance with standards established by the American Institute of CPAs

    C. the accountant has not audited or reviewed the financial statements

    D. the accountant does not express an opinion but expresses only limited assurance on the financial statements

12. Which of the following should be included in an accoun-    12.___
tant's standard report based upon the review of a non-public entity's financial statements? A statement that

    A. the review was performed in accordance with generally accepted review standards

    B. a review consists principally of inquiries and analytical procedures

    C. the accountant is independent with respect to the entity

    D. a review is substantially greater in scope than a compilation

13. When the financial statements contain a departure from generally accepted accounting principles, the effect of which is material, the auditor should

    A. qualify the opinion and explain the effect of the departure from generally accepted accounting principles in a separate paragraph

    B. qualify the opinion and describe the departure from generally accepted accounting principles within the opinion paragraph

    C. disclaim an opinion and explain the effect of the departure from generally accepted accounting principles in a separate paragraph

    D. disclaim an opinion and describe the departure from generally accepted accounting principles within the opinion paragraph

13.___

14. The third standard of field work states that sufficient competent evidential matter may, in part, be obtained through inspection, observation, inquiries, and confirmations to afford a reasonable basis for an opinion regarding the financial statements under examination.
The evidential matter required by this standard may, in part, be obtained through

    A. analytical review procedures

    B. auditor working papers

    C. review of the system of internal accounting control

    D. proper planning of the audit engagement

14.___

15. The auditor should consider expressing a *subject to* qualified opinion when

    A. the auditor is prevented from completing a procedure required by generally accepted auditing standards

    B. the financial statements fail to disclose information required by generally accepted accounting principles

    C. the auditor decides to make reference to the report of another auditor

    D. a question arises about the entity's continued existence

15.___

16. Management of Blue Company has decided not to account for a material transaction in accordance with the provisions of an FASB Standard. In setting forth its reasons in a note to the financial statements, management has clearly demonstrated that due to unusual circumstances the financial statements presented in accordance with the FASB Standard would be misleading.
The auditor's report should include an explanatory separate paragraph and contain a(n) _____ opinion.

    A. adverse              B. unqualified

    C. *except for* qualified    D. *subject to* qualified

16.___

17. Auditors who prefer statistical sampling to non-statistical sampling may do so because statistical sampling helps the auditor
    A. measure the sufficiency of the evidential matter obtained
    B. eliminate subjectivity in the evaluation of sampling results
    C. reduce the level of tolerable error to a relatively low amount
    D. minimize the failure to detect a material misstatement due to nonsampling risk

17.___

18. Confirmation is MOST likely to be a relevant form of evidence with regard to assertions about accounts receivable when the auditor has concerns about the receivables'
    A. valuation                B. classification
    C. existence                D. completeness

18.___

19. Before performing a compilation of the financial statements of a nonpublic entity, an accountant should
    A. perform a thorough study and evaluation of the internal accounting control system
    B. complete a series of inquiries concerning the entity's procedures for recording, classifying, and summarizing transactions
    C. design working papers intended to provide sufficient competent evidential matter to afford a reasonable basis for a compilation opinion
    D. obtain an understanding of the accounting principles and practices of the industry in which the entity operates

19.___

20. After issuing a report, an auditor concludes that an auditing procedure considered necessary at the time of the examination was omitted from the examination.
    The auditor should FIRST
    A. undertake to apply the omitted procedure or alternative procedures that would provide a satisfactory basis for the auditor's opinion
    B. assess the importance of the omitted procedure to the auditor's ability to support the opinion expressed on the financial statements taken as a whole
    C. notify the audit committee or the board of directors that the auditor's opinion can no longer be relied upon
    D. review the results of other procedures that were applied to compensate for the one omitted or to make its omission less important

20.___

21. An auditor issued an audit report that was dual dated for a subsequent event occurring after the completion of field work but before issuance of the auditor's report. The auditor's responsibility for events occurring subsequent to the completion of field work was

21.___

A. limited to the specific event referenced
B. limited to include only events occurring before the date of the last subsequent event referenced
C. extended to subsequent events occurring through the date of issuance of the report
D. extended to include all events occurring since the completion of field work

22. Which of the following might be detected by an auditor's review of the client's sales cut-off?  22.___
    A. Excessive goods returned for credit
    B. Unrecorded sales discounts
    C. Lapping of year-end accounts receivable
    D. Inflated sales for the year

23. An auditor would be MOST likely to identify a contingent liability by obtaining a(n) _____ confirmation.  23.___
    A. related party transaction
    B. accounts payable
    C. transfer agent
    D. standard bank

24. Which of the following sampling plans would be designed to estimate a numerical measurement of a population, such as a dollar value?  24.___
    A. Discovery sampling
    B. Numerical sampling
    C. Sampling for variables
    D. Sampling for attributes

25. Processing simulated file data provides the auditor with information about the reliability of controls from evidence that exists in simulated files.
    One of the techniques involved in this approach makes use of  25.___
    A. controlled reprocessing
    B. program code checking
    C. printout reviews
    D. integrated test facility

26. The LEAST likely use by the auditor of generalized audit software is to  26.___
    A. perform analytical review on the client's data
    B. access the information stored on the client's EDP files
    C. identify weaknesses in the client's EDP controls
    D. test the accuracy of the client's computations

27. The auditor's PRIMARY means of obtaining corroboration of management's information concerning litigation is a  27.___
    A. letter of audit inquiry to the client's lawyer
    B. letter of corroboration from the auditor's lawyer upon review of the legal documentation
    C. confirmation of claims and assessments from the other parties to the litigation
    D. confirmation of claims and assessments from an officer of the court presiding over the litigation

28. The concept of materiality would be LEAST important to an auditor when considering the    28.___
    A. decision whether to use positive or negative confirmations of accounts receivable
    B. adequacy of disclosure of a client's illegal act
    C. discovery of weaknesses in a client's internal accounting control
    D. effects of a direct financial interest in the client upon the CPA's independence

29. Hall accepted an engagement to audit the 1991 financial    29.___
    statements of XYZ Company. XYZ completed the preparation
    of the 1991 financial statements on February 13, 1992,
    and Hall began the field work on February 17, 1992. Hall
    completed the field work on March 24, 1992 and completed
    the report on March 28, 1992.
    The client's representation letter normally would be dated
    A. February 13, 1992          B. February 17, 1992
    C. March 24, 1992             D. March 28, 1992

30. When an auditor is unable to inspect and count a client's    30.___
    investment securities until after the balance sheet date,
    the bank where the securities are held in a safe deposit
    box should be asked to
    A. verify any differences between the contents of the box and the balances in the client's subsidiary ledger
    B. provide a list of securities added and removed from the box between the balance sheet date and the security-count date
    C. confirm that there has been no access to the box between the balance sheet date and the security-count date
    D. count the securities in the box so the auditor will have an independent direct verification

---

# KEY (CORRECT ANSWERS)

| | | |
|---|---|---|
| 1. C | 11. D | 21. A |
| 2. A | 12. B | 22. D |
| 3. C | 13. A | 23. D |
| 4. B | 14. A | 24. C |
| 5. A | 15. D | 25. D |
| 6. A | 16. B | 26. C |
| 7. C | 17. A | 27. A |
| 8. D | 18. C | 28. D |
| 9. C | 19. D | 29. C |
| 10. A | 20. B | 30. C |

# TEST 2

DIRECTIONS: Each question or incomplete statement is followed by several suggested answers or completions. Select the one that BEST answers the question or completes the statement.

1. An aged trial balance of accounts receivable is USUALLY used by the auditor to
   A. verify the validity of recorded receivables
   B. ensure that all accounts are promptly credited
   C. evaluate the results of compliance tests
   D. evaluate the provision for bad debt expense

1.___

2. Which of the following audit procedures would provide the LEAST reliable evidence that the client has legal title to inventories?
   A. Confirmation of inventories at locations outside the client's facilities
   B. Analytical review of inventory balances compared to purchasing and sales activities
   C. Observation of physical inventory counts
   D. Examination of paid vendors' invoices

2.___

3. The auditor's analytical review will be facilitated if the client
   A. uses a standard cost system that produces variance reports
   B. segregates obsolete inventory before the physical inventory count
   C. corrects material weaknesses in internal accounting control before the beginning of the audit
   D. reduces inventory balances to the lower of cost or market

3.___

4. Which of the following statements with respect to the auditor's required communication of a material weakness in internal accounting control is CORRECT?
   A. A weakness discovered should be compliance tested by the auditor before being communicated to the client.
   B. Suggested corrective action for management's consideration with respect to a weakness need not be communicated to the client.
   C. A weakness previously communicated during prior years' audits that has not been corrected need not be communicated again.
   D. The communication of a weakness for which management believes corrective action is not practicable should be included in a separate paragraph of the auditor's report.

4.___

5. Which of the following procedures is USUALLY included in
   a review engagement of a nonpublic entity?
   A. The confirmation of accounts receivable
   B. A study and evaluation of internal accounting control
   C. An inquiry concerning subsequent events
   D. The observation of physical inventory counts

5.___

6. A BASIC premise underlying analytical review procedures
   is that
   A. statistical tests of financial information may lead
      to the discovery of material errors in the financial
      statements
   B. the study of financial ratios is an acceptable alter-
      native to the investigation of unusual fluctuations
   C. relationships among data may reasonably be expected
      to exist and continue in the absence of known con-
      ditions to the contrary
   D. these procedures cannot replace tests of balances
      and transactions

6.___

7. Which of the following is a question that the auditor
   would expect to find on the production cycle section of
   an internal accounting control questionnaire?
   Are
   A. vendors' invoices for raw materials approved for
      payment by an employee who is independent of the
      cash disbursements function?
   B. signed checks for the purchase of raw materials
      mailed directly after signing without being returned
      to the person who authorized the invoice processing?
   C. all releases by storekeepers of raw materials from
      storage based on approved requisition documents?
   D. details of individual disbursements for raw materials
      balanced with the total to be posted to the appro-
      priate general ledger account?

7.___

8. For the accounting system of Acme Company, the amounts of
   cash disbursements entered into an EDP terminal are trans-
   mitted to the computer that immediately transmits the
   amounts back to the terminal for display on the terminal
   screen.
   This display enables the operator to
   A. establish the validity of the account number
   B. verify the amount was entered accurately
   C. verify the authorization of the disbursement
   D. prevent the overpayment of the account

8.___

9. To determine whether the system of internal accounting
   control operated effectively to minimize errors of failure
   to invoice a shipment, the auditor would select a sample
   of transactions from the population represented by the
   _____ file.
   A. customer order            B. bill of lading
   C. open invoice              D. sales invoice

9.___

10. In the examination of the financial statements of Delta       10.___
    Company, the auditor determines that in performing a
    compliance test of internal accounting control, the
    compliance rate in the sample does not support the planned
    degree of reliance on the control when, in fact, the
    compliance rate in the population does justify such
    reliance.
    This situation illustrates the risk of
       A. overreliance              B. underreliance
       C. incorrect rejection       D. incorrect acceptance

11. When performing a compliance test with respect to control    11.___
    over cash receipts, an auditor may use a systematic
    sampling technique with a start at any randomly selected
    item.
    The BIGGEST disadvantage of this type of sampling is that
    the items in the population
       A. must be systematically replaced in the population
          after sampling
       B. may systematically occur more than once in the sample
       C. must be recorded in a systematic pattern before the
          sample can be drawn
       D. may occur in a systematic pattern, thus destroying
          the sample randomness

12. After finishing the review of the design of the internal     12.___
    accounting control system in an audit engagement, the
    auditor should perform compliance tests on
       A. those controls that have a material effect upon the
          financial statement balances
       B. a random sample of the controls that were reviewed
       C. those controls that the auditor plans to rely upon
       D. those controls in which material weaknesses were
          identified

13. Which of the following is a provision of the Foreign         13.___
    Corrupt Practices Act?
       A. It is a criminal offense for an auditor to fail to
          detect and report a bribe paid by an American business
          entity to a foreign official for the purpose of
          obtaining business.
       B. The auditor's detection of illegal acts committed by
          officials of the auditor's publicly held client in
          conjunction with foreign officials should be reported
          to the Enforcement Division of the Securities and
          Exchange Commission.
       C. If the auditor of a publicly held company concludes
          that the effects on the financial statements of a
          bribe given to a foreign official are not susceptible
          of reasonable estimation, the auditor's report should
          be modified.
       D. Every publicly held company must devise, document,
          and maintain a system of internal accounting controls
          sufficient to provide reasonable assurances that
          internal accounting control objectives are met.

14. After completing all compliance testing, the auditor     14.___
    should review the results and consider whether
    A. the planned degree of reliance on the internal
       accounting controls is justified
    B. the evidential matter obtained from the study of the
       internal accounting controls can provide a reasonable
       basis for an opinion
    C. further study of the internal accounting controls is
       likely to justify any restriction of substantive
       tests
    D. sufficient knowledge has been obtained about the
       entity's entire internal accounting control system

15. When an accountant is NOT independent of a client and is     15.___
    requested to perform a compilation of its financial
    statements, the accountant
    A. is precluded from accepting the engagement
    B. may accept the engagement and need not disclose the
       lack of independence
    C. may accept the engagement and should disclose the
       lack of independence but not the reason for the lack
       of independence
    D. may accept the engagement and should disclose both
       the lack of independence and the reason for the lack
       of independence

Questions 16-17.

DIRECTIONS:   Questions 16 and 17 are to be answered on the basis
              of the following information.

During the annual audit of BCD Corp., a publicly held company,
Smith, CPA, a continuing auditor, determined that illegal political
contributions had been made during each of the past seven years,
including the year under audit.  Smith notified the board of
directors of BCD Corp. of the illegal contributions, but they
refused to take any action because the amounts involved were immaterial to the financial statements.

16. Since management took no action, Smith should     16.___
    A. report the illegal contributions to the Securities
       and Exchange Commission
    B. issue an *except for* qualified opinion or an adverse
       opinion
    C. disregard the political contributions since the board
       of directors were notified and the amounts involved
       were immaterial
    D. consider withdrawing from the engagement or dissoci-
       ating from any future relationship with BCD Corp.

17. Smith should reconsider the intended degree of reliance     17.___
    to be placed on the
    A. management representation letter
    B. preliminary judgment about materiality levels
    C. letter of audit inquiry to the client's attorney
    D. prior years' audit programs

18. A secondary objective of the auditor's study and evalua-  18.___
    tion of internal accounting control is that the study
    and evaluation provide
    A. a basis for determining the nature, extent, and
       timing of audit tests
    B. assurance that management's procedures to detect
       irregularities are properly functioning
    C. a basis for constructive suggestions concerning
       improvements in internal accounting control
    D. evidence that incompatible functions for accounting
       control purposes have been eliminated

19. Which of the following is NOT required by the generally  19.___
    accepted auditing standard that states that due profes-
    sional care is to be exercised in the performance of the
    examination?
    A. Observance of the standards of field work and
       reporting
    B. Critical review of the audit work performed at every
       level of supervision
    C. Degree of skill commonly possessed by others in the
       profession
    D. Responsibility for losses because of errors of
       judgment

20. A basic objective of a CPA firm is to provide profession-  20.___
    al services that conform with professional standards.
    Reasonable assurance of achieving this basic objective
    is provided through
    A. a system of peer review
    B. continuing professional education
    C. a system of quality control
    D. compliance with generally accepted reporting
       standards

21. Prior to beginning the field work on a new audit engage-  21.___
    ment in which a CPA does not possess expertise in the
    industry in which the client operates, the CPA should
    A. reduce audit risk by lowering the preliminary levels
       of materiality
    B. design special substantive tests to compensate for
       the lack of industry expertise
    C. engage financial experts familiar with the nature
       of the industry
    D. obtain a knowledge of matters that relate to the
       nature of the entity's business

22. When one auditor succeeds another, the successor auditor  22.___
    should request the
    A. client to instruct its attorney to send a letter of
       audit inquiry concerning the status of the prior
       year's litigation, claims, and assessments
    B. predecessor auditor to submit a list of internal
       accounting control weaknesses that have not been
       corrected

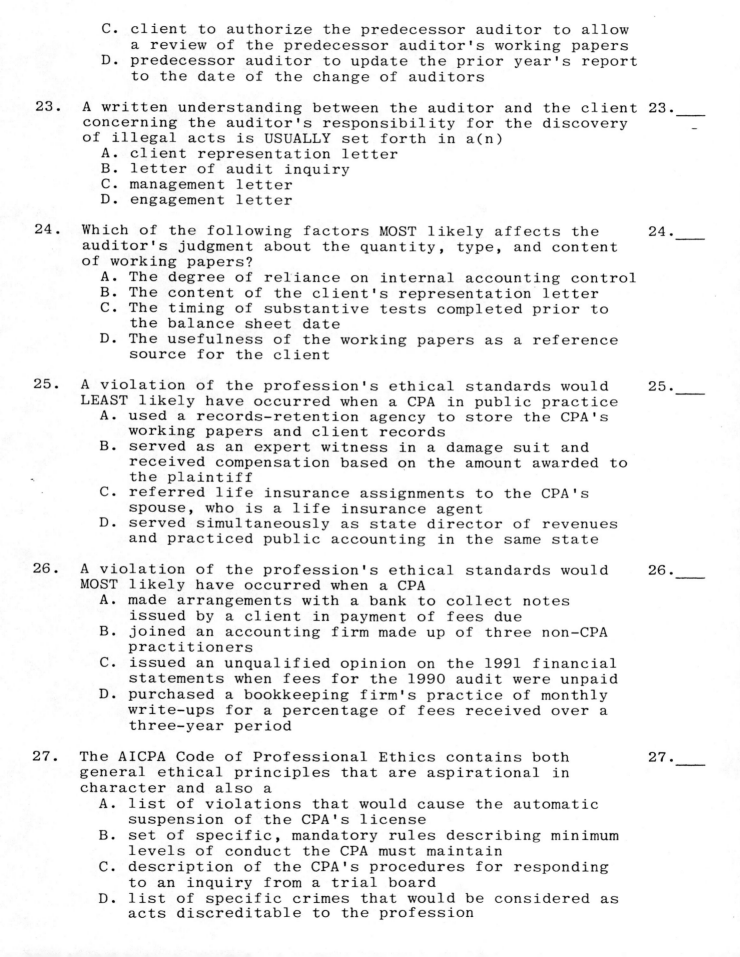

    C. client to authorize the predecessor auditor to allow
       a review of the predecessor auditor's working papers
    D. predecessor auditor to update the prior year's report
       to the date of the change of auditors

23. A written understanding between the auditor and the client  23.___
    concerning the auditor's responsibility for the discovery
    of illegal acts is USUALLY set forth in a(n)
    A. client representation letter
    B. letter of audit inquiry
    C. management letter
    D. engagement letter

24. Which of the following factors MOST likely affects the  24.___
    auditor's judgment about the quantity, type, and content
    of working papers?
    A. The degree of reliance on internal accounting control
    B. The content of the client's representation letter
    C. The timing of substantive tests completed prior to
       the balance sheet date
    D. The usefulness of the working papers as a reference
       source for the client

25. A violation of the profession's ethical standards would  25.___
    LEAST likely have occurred when a CPA in public practice
    A. used a records-retention agency to store the CPA's
       working papers and client records
    B. served as an expert witness in a damage suit and
       received compensation based on the amount awarded to
       the plaintiff
    C. referred life insurance assignments to the CPA's
       spouse, who is a life insurance agent
    D. served simultaneously as state director of revenues
       and practiced public accounting in the same state

26. A violation of the profession's ethical standards would  26.___
    MOST likely have occurred when a CPA
    A. made arrangements with a bank to collect notes
       issued by a client in payment of fees due
    B. joined an accounting firm made up of three non-CPA
       practitioners
    C. issued an unqualified opinion on the 1991 financial
       statements when fees for the 1990 audit were unpaid
    D. purchased a bookkeeping firm's practice of monthly
       write-ups for a percentage of fees received over a
       three-year period

27. The AICPA Code of Professional Ethics contains both  27.___
    general ethical principles that are aspirational in
    character and also a
    A. list of violations that would cause the automatic
       suspension of the CPA's license
    B. set of specific, mandatory rules describing minimum
       levels of conduct the CPA must maintain
    C. description of the CPA's procedures for responding
       to an inquiry from a trial board
    D. list of specific crimes that would be considered as
       acts discreditable to the profession

28. Under Statements on Auditing Standards, which of the
    following would be classified as an error?
    A. Misappropriation of assets for the benefit of
       management
    B. Misinterpretation by management of facts that
       existed when the financial statements were prepared
    C. Preparation of records by employees to cover a
       fraudulent scheme
    D. Intentional omission of the recording of a trans-
       action to benefit a third party

    28. ___

29. When using the work of a specialist, the auditor may
    make reference to and identification of the specialist
    in the auditor's report if the
    A. auditor decides to express a qualified opinion
    B. specialist's reputation or professional certification
       is being emphasized
    C. auditor wishes to indicate a division of responsi-
       bility
    D. specialist's work provides the auditor greater
       assurance of reliability

    29. ___

30. As guidance for measuring the quality of the performance
    of an auditor, the auditor should refer to
    A. Statements of the Financial Accounting Standards
       Board
    B. generally accepted auditing standards
    C. interpretations of the Statements on Auditing
       Standards
    D. Statements on Quality Control Standards

    30. ___

# KEY (CORRECT ANSWERS)

| | | |
|---|---|---|
| 1. D | 11. D | 21. D |
| 2. B | 12. C | 22. C |
| 3. A | 13. D | 23. D |
| 4. B | 14. A | 24. A |
| 5. C | 15. C | 25. A |
| 6. C | 16. D | 26. C |
| 7. C | 17. A | 27. B |
| 8. B | 18. C | 28. B |
| 9. B | 19. D | 29. A |
| 10. B | 20. C | 30. B |

# EXAMINATION SECTION
## TEST 1

DIRECTIONS:  Each question or incomplete statement is followed by several suggested answers or completions. Select the one that BEST answers the question or completes the statement. *PRINT THE LETTER OF THE CORRECT ANSWER IN THE SPACE AT THE RIGHT.*

1.  If an auditor believes there is minimal likelihood that resolution of an uncertainty will have a material effect on the financial statements, the auditor should issue a(n) _____ opinion.

    A.  unqualified  
    B.  disclaimer of  
    C.  *except for* qualified  
    D.  *subject to* qualified

1.____

2.  Which of the following BEST describes the auditor's reporting responsibility concerning information accompanying the basic financial statements in an auditor-submitted document?  
The auditor should report on

    A.  all the information included in the document  
    B.  the basic financial statements but may not issue a report covering the accompanying information  
    C.  the information accompanying the basic financial statements only if the auditor participated in the preparation of the accompanying information  
    D.  the information accompanying the basic financial statements only if the document is being distributed to public shareholders

2.____

3.  Which of the following are prospective financial statements upon which an accountant may appropriately report for general use?

    A.  Pro forma financial statements  
    B.  Financial projections  
    C.  Partial presentations  
    D.  Financial forecasts

3.____

4.  Given one or more hypothetical assumptions, a responsible party may prepare, to the best of its knowledge and belief, an entity's expected financial position, results of operations, and changes in financial position.  
Such prospective financial statements are known as

    A.  Pro forma financial statements  
    B.  Financial projections  
    C.  Partial presentations  
    D.  Financial forecasts

4.____

5.  Subsequent to the issuance of the auditor's report, the auditor became aware of facts existing at the report date that would have affected the report had the auditor then been aware of such facts.  
After determining that the information is reliable, the auditor should NEXT

5.____

   A.  notify the board of directors that the auditor's report must no longer be associated with the financial statements
   B.  determine whether there are persons relying or likely to rely on the financial statements who would attach importance to the information
   C.  request that management disclose the effects of the newly discovered information by adding a footnote to subsequently issued financial statements
   D.  issue revised pro forma financial statements taking into consideration the newly discovered information

6.  When an auditor reports on financial statements prepared on an entity's income tax basis, the auditor's report should    6.__

   A.  disclose that the statements are not intended to conform with generally accepted accounting principles
   B.  disclaim an opinion on whether the statements were examined in accordance with generally accepted auditing standards
   C.  not express an opinion on whether the statements are presented in conformity with the comprehensive basis of accounting used
   D.  include an explanation of how the results of operations differ from the cash receipts and disbursements basis of accounting

7.  When reporting on comparative financial statements where the financial statements of the prior period have been examined by a predecessor auditor whose report is not presented, the successor auditor should indicate in the scope paragraph    7.__

   A.  the reasons why the predecessor auditor's report is not presented
   B.  the identity of the predecessor auditor who examined the financial statements of the prior year
   C.  whether the predecessor auditor's review of the current year's financial statements revealed any matters that might have a material effect on the successor auditor's opinion
   D.  the type of opinion expressed by the predecessor auditor

8.  The auditor would MOST likely issue a disclaimer of opinion because of    8.__

   A.  the client's failure to present supplementary information required by the FASB
   B.  inadequate disclosure of material information
   C.  a client imposed scope limitation
   D.  the qualification of an opinion by the other auditor of a subsidiary where there is a division of responsibility

9.  The principal auditor is satisfied with the independence and professional reputation of the other auditor who has audited a subsidiary but wants to indicate the division of responsibility.
The principal auditor should    9.__

   A.  modify only the scope paragraph of the report
   B.  modify only the opinion paragraph of the report
   C.  modify both the scope and opinion paragraphs of the report
   D.  not modify the report except for inclusion of a separate explanatory paragraph

10. The management of a client company believes that the statement of changes in financial    10.____
position (statement of cash flows) is not a useful document and refuses to include one in
the annual report to stockholders.
As a result of this circumstance, the auditor's opinion should be

    A.  adverse
    B.  unqualified
    C.  qualified due to inadequate disclosure
    D.  qualified due to a scope limitation

11. When an auditor qualifies an opinion because of a scope limitation, which paragraph(s)    11.____
of the auditor's report should indicate that the qualification pertains to the possible effects
on the financial statements and not to the scope limitation itself?

    A.  The scope paragraph and the separate explanatory paragraph
    B.  The separate explanatory paragraph and the opinion paragraph
    C.  The scope paragraph *only*
    D.  The opinion paragraph *only*

12. When an independent accountant's report based on a review of interim financial informa-    12.____
tion is incorporated by reference in a registration statement, the Securities and Exchange
Commission requires that the prospectus clarify that the accountant's report is NOT

    A.  a part of the registration statement within the meaning of the Securities Act of 1933
    B.  subject to the Statements on Standards for Accounting and Review Services
    C.  to be relied upon due to the limited nature of the procedures applied
    D.  included in the company's quarterly report on Form 10-Q

13. A client acquired 25% of its outstanding capital stock after year-end and prior to comple-    13.____
tion of the auditor's field work.
The auditor should

    A.  advise management to adjust the balance sheet to reflect the acquisition
    B.  issue pro forma financial statements giving effect to the acquisition as if it had
        occurred at year-end
    C.  advise management to disclose the acquisition in the notes to the financial state-
        ments
    D.  disclose the acquisition in the opinion paragraph of the auditor's report

14. An auditor concludes that an audit procedure considered necessary at the time of the    14.____
examination had been omitted. The auditor should assess the importance of the omitted
procedure to the ability to support the previously expressed opinion.
Which of the following would be LEAST helpful in making that assessment?

    A.  A discussion with the client about whether there are persons relying on the audi-
        tor's report
    B.  A reevaluation of the overall scope of the examination
    C.  A discussion of the circumstances with engagement personnel
    D.  A review of the other audit procedures that were applied that might compensate for
        the one omitted

15. Which of the following statements concerning the auditor's use of the work of a specialist   15.___
is CORRECT?

    A. If the specialist is related to the client, the auditor is not permitted to use the specialist's findings as corroborative evidence.
    B. The specialist may be identified in the auditor's report only when the auditor issues a qualified opinion.
    C. The specialist should have an understanding of the auditor's corroborative use of the specialist's findings.
    D. If the auditor believes that the determinations made by the specialist are unreasonable, only an adverse opinion may be issued.

16. When using a computer to gather evidence, the auditor need not have working knowl-   16.___
edge of the client's programming language.
However, it is necessary that the auditor understand the

    A. audit specifications
    B. programming techniques
    C. database retrieval system
    D. manual testing techniques

17. Which of the following is NOT a major reason why an accounting audit trail should be   17.___
maintained for a computer system?

    A. Query answering
    B. Deterrent to irregularities
    C. Monitoring purposes
    D. Analytical review

18. Working papers that record the procedures used by the auditor to gather evidence   18.___
should be

    A. considered the primary support for the financial statements being examined
    B. viewed as the connecting link between the books of account and the financial statements
    C. designed to meet the circumstances of the particular engagement
    D. destroyed when the audited entity ceases to be a client

19. If the financial statements, including accompanying notes, fail to disclose information that   19.___
is required by generally accepted accounting principles, the auditor should express either
a(n)

    A. *except for* qualified opinion or an adverse opinion
    B. adverse opinion or a *subject to* qualified opinion
    C. *subject to* qualified opinion or an unqualified opinion with a separate explanatory paragraph
    D. unqualified opinion with a separate explanatory paragraph or an *except for* qualified opinion

20. If there were no changes during the reporting period in the application of accounting prin-   20.___
ciples, which of the following types of opinions should omit any reference to consistency?
_____ opinion.

    A. *except for* qualified              B. unqualified
    C. *subject to* qualified             D. adverse

21. A limitation on the scope of the auditor's examination sufficient to preclude an unqualified opinion will ALWAYS result when management 21.____

    A. prevents the auditor from reviewing the working papers of the predecessor auditor
    B. engages the auditor after the year-end physical inventory count is completed
    C. fails to correct a material internal accounting control weakness that had been identified during the prior year's audit
    D. refuses to furnish a management representation letter to the auditor

22. Operational auditing is PRIMARILY oriented toward 22.____

    A. future improvements to accomplish the goals of management
    B. the accuracy of data reflected in management's financial records
    C. the verification that a company's financial statements are fairly presented
    D. past protection provided by existing internal accounting control

23. Which of the following is the BEST audit procedure for determining the existence of unrecorded liabilities at year-end?
Examine 23.____

    A. a sample of invoices dated a few days prior to and subsequent to year-end to ascertain whether they have been properly recorded
    B. a sample of cash disbursements in the period subsequent to year-end
    C. confirmation requests returned by creditors whose accounts appear on a subsidiary trial balance of accounts payable
    D. unusual relationships between monthly accounts payable balances and recorded purchases

24. An auditor ordinarily should send a standard confirmation request to all banks with which the client has done business during the year under audit, regardless of the year-end balance, because this procedure 24.____

    A. provides for confirmation regarding compensating balance arrangements
    B. detects kiting activities that may otherwise not be discovered
    C. seeks information about indebtedness to the bank
    D. verifies securities held by the bank in safekeeping

25. On receiving the bank cutoff statement, the auditor should trace 25.____

    A. deposits in transit on the year-end bank reconciliation to deposits in the cash receipts journal
    B. checks dated prior to year-end to the outstanding checks listed on the year-end bank reconciliation
    C. deposits listed on the cutoff statement to deposits in the cash receipts journal
    D. checks dated subsequent to year-end to the outstanding checks listed on the year-end bank reconciliations

26. Which of the following would the accountant MOST likely investigate during the review of financial statements of a nonpublic entity if accounts receivable did not conform to a predictable pattern during the year? 26.____

    A. Sales returns and allowances     B. Credit sales
    C. Sales of consigned goods     D. Cash sales

27. Prior to commencing the compilation of financial statements of a nonpublic entity, the accountant should

    A. perform analytical review procedures sufficient to determine whether fluctuations among account balances appear reasonable
    B. complete the preliminary phase of the study and evaluation of the entity's internal accounting control
    C. verify that the financial information supplied by the entity agrees with the books of original entry
    D. acquire a knowledge of any specialized accounting principles and practices used in the entity's industry

27.__

28. After discovering that a related party transaction exists, the auditor should be aware that the

    A. substance of the transaction could be significantly different from its form
    B. adequacy of disclosure of the transaction is secondary to its legal form
    C. transaction is assumed to be outside the ordinary course of business
    D. financial statements should recognize the legal form of the transaction rather than its substance

28.__

29. Which of the following auditing procedures is ordinarily performed LAST?

    A. Obtaining a management representation letter
    B. Testing the purchasing function
    C. Reading the minutes of directors' meetings
    D. Confirming accounts payable

29.__

30. Which of the following is the MOST effective audit procedure for verification of dividends earned on investments in marketable equity securities?

    A. Tracing deposit of dividend checks to the cash receipts book
    B. Reconciling amounts received with published dividend records
    C. Comparing the amounts received with preceding year dividends received
    D. Recomputing selected extensions and footings of dividend schedules and comparing totals to the general ledger

30.__

# KEY (CORRECT ANSWERS)

| | | | | |
|---|---|---|---|---|
| 1. | A | | 16. | A |
| 2. | A | | 17. | D |
| 3. | D | | 18. | C |
| 4. | B | | 19. | A |
| 5. | B | | 20. | D |
| 6. | A | | 21. | D |
| 7. | D | | 22. | A |
| 8. | C | | 23. | B |
| 9. | C | | 24. | C |
| 10. | C | | 25. | B |
| 11. | D | | 26. | B |
| 12. | A | | 27. | D |
| 13. | C | | 28. | A |
| 14. | A | | 29. | A |
| 15. | C | | 30. | B |

———

# TEST 2

DIRECTIONS: Each question or incomplete statement is followed by several suggested answers or completions. Select the one that BEST answers the question or completes the statement. *PRINT THE LETTER OF THE CORRECT ANSWER IN THE SPACE AT THE RIGHT.*

1. When auditing merchandise inventory at year-end, the auditor performs a purchase cut-off test to obtain evidence that    1.__

    A. all goods purchased before year-end are received before the physical inventory count
    B. no goods held on consignment for customers are included in the inventory balance
    C. no goods observed during the physical count are pledged or sold
    D. all goods owned at year-end are included in the inventory balance

2. Without the consent of the client, a CPA should NOT disclose confidential client information contained in working papers to a    2.__

    A. voluntary quality control review board
    B. CPA firm that has purchased the CPA's accounting practice
    C. federal court that has issued a valid subpoena
    D. disciplinary body created under state statute

3. An example of an analytical review procedure is the comparison of    3.__

    A. financial information with similar information regarding the industry in which the entity operates
    B. recorded amounts of major disbursements with appropriate invoices
    C. results of a statistical sample with the expected characteristics of the actual population
    D. EDP generated data with similar data generated by a manual accounting system

4. Audit evidence can come in different forms with different degrees of persuasiveness. Which of the following is the LEAST persuasive type of evidence?    4.__

    A. Bank statement obtained from the client
    B. Computations made by the auditor
    C. Prenumbered client sales invoices
    D. Vendor's invoice

Questions 5-7.

DIRECTIONS: Questions 5 through 7 are to be answered on the basis of the following section of a system flowchart for a payroll application.

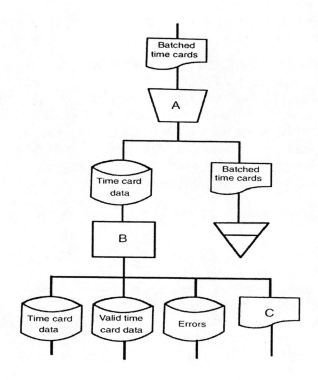

5. Symbol C could represent

    A.  batched time cards
    B.  unclaimed payroll checks
    C.  erroneous time cards
    D.  an error report

5._____

6. Symbol B could represent

    A.  computation of net pay
    B.  separation of erroneous time cards
    C.  validation of payroll data
    D.  preparation of the payroll register

6._____

7. Symbol A could represent

    A.  computation of gross pay
    B.  input of payroll data
    C.  preparation of paychecks
    D.  verification of payrates

7._____

8. When there are a large number of relatively small account balances, negative confirmation of accounts receivable is feasible if internal accounting control is _____ and the individuals receiving the confirmation requests are _____ to give them adequate consideration.

    A.  strong; unlikely        B.  weak; likely
    C.  weak; unlikely        D.  strong; likely

8._____

9.  When there are few property and equipment transactions during the year, the continuing auditor USUALLY makes a    9.__

   A.   complete review of the related internal accounting controls and performs compliance tests of those controls being relied upon
   B.   complete review of the related internal accounting controls and performs analytical review tests to verify current year additions to property and equipment
   C.   preliminary review of the related internal accounting controls and performs a thorough examination of the balances at the beginning of the year
   D.   preliminary review of the related internal accounting controls and performs extensive tests of current year property and equipment transactions

10.  A weakness in internal accounting control over recording retirements of equipment may cause the auditor to    10.__

   A.   inspect certain items of equipment in the plant and trace those items to the accounting records
   B.   review the subsidiary ledger to ascertain whether depreciation was taken on each item of equipment during the year
   C.   trace additions to the *other assets* account to search for equipment that is still on hand but no longer being used
   D.   select certain items of equipment from the accounting records and locate them in the plant

11.  The auditor may observe the distribution of paychecks to ascertain whether    11.__

   A.   payrate authorization is properly separated from the operating function
   B.   deductions from gross pay are calculated correctly and are properly authorized
   C.   employees of record actually exist and are employed by the client
   D.   paychecks agree with the payroll register and the time cards

12.  The auditor's communication of material weaknesses in internal accounting control is    12.__

   A.   required to enable the auditor to state that the examination has been made in accordance with generally accepted auditing standards
   B.   the principal reason for studying and evaluating the system of internal accounting controls
   C.   incident to the auditor's objective of forming an opinion as to the fair presentation of the financial statements
   D.   required to be documented in a written report to the board of directors or the board's audit committee

13.  The purpose of segregating the duties of hiring personnel and distributing payroll checks is to separate the    13.__

   A.   operational responsibility from the record keeping responsibility
   B.   responsibilities of recording a transaction at its origin from the ultimate posting in the general ledger
   C.   authorization of transactions from the custody of related assets
   D.   human resources function from the controllership function

14. Which of the following internal accounting control procedures could BEST prevent direct labor from being charged to manufacturing overhead?

    A. Reconciliation of work in process inventory with cost records
    B. Comparison of daily journal entries with factory labor summary
    C. Comparison of periodic cost budgets and time cards
    D. Reconciliation of unfinished job summary and production cost records

14.____

15. Instead of taking a physical inventory count on the balance-sheet date, the client may take physical counts prior to the year-end if internal accounting controls are adequate and

    A. computerized records of perpetual inventory are maintained
    B. inventory is slow-moving
    C. EDP error reports are generated for missing pre-numbered inventory tickets
    D. obsolete inventory items are segregated and excluded

15.____

16. In a properly designed internal accounting control system, the same employee may be permitted to

    A. receive and deposit checks, and also approve writeoffs of customer accounts
    B. approve vouchers for payment, and also sign checks
    C. reconcile the bank statements, and also receive and deposit cash
    D. sign checks, and also cancel supporting documents

16.____

17. An internal accounting control questionnaire indicates that an approved receiving report is required to accompany every check request for payment of merchandise.
Which of the following procedures provides the GREATEST assurance that this control is operating effectively?
Select and examine

    A. cancelled checks and ascertain that the related receiving reports are dated no earlier than the checks
    B. cancelled checks and ascertain that the related receiving reports are dated no later than the checks
    C. receiving reports and ascertain that the related cancelled checks are dated no earlier than the receiving reports
    D. receiving reports and ascertain that the related cancelled checks are dated no later than the receiving reports

17.____

18. The completeness of EDP-generated sales figures can be tested by comparing the number of items listed on the daily sales report with the number of items billed on the actual invoices.
This process uses

    A. check digits
    C. validity tests
    B. control totals
    D. process tracing data

18.____

19. For effective internal accounting control, employees maintaining the accounts receivable subsidiary ledger should NOT also approve

    A. employee overtime wages
    B. credit granted to customers
    C. write-offs of customer accounts
    D. cash disbursements

19.____

20. Based on a study and evaluation completed at an interim date, the auditor concludes that 20.__
no significant internal accounting control weaknesses exist.
The records and procedures would MOST likely be tested again at year-end if

    A. compliance tests were not performed by the internal auditor during the remaining period

    B. the internal accounting control system provides a basis for reliance in reducing the extent of substantive testing

    C. the auditor used nonstatistical sampling during the interim period compliance testing

    D. inquiries and observations lead the auditor to believe that conditions have changed

21. After completing the preliminary phase of the review of internal accounting control, the 21.__
auditor decides not to rely on the system to restrict substantive tests. Documentation
may be limited to the auditor's

    A. understanding of the internal accounting control system

    B. reasons for deciding not to extend the review

    C. basis for concluding that errors and irregularities will be prevented

    D. completed internal accounting control questionnaire

Question 22.

DIRECTIONS: Question 22 is to be answered on the basis of the following diagram, which depicts the auditor's estimated deviation rate compared with the tolerable rate, and also depicts the true population deviation rate compared with the tolerable rate.

| Auditor's Estimate Based on Sample Results | True State of Population | |
|---|---|---|
| | Deviation Rate Exceeds Tolerable Rate | Deviation Rate is Less Than Tolerable Rate |
| Deviation Rate Exceeds Tolerable Rate | I. | III. |
| Deviation Rate is Less Than Tolerable Rate | II. | IV. |

22. As a result of compliance testing, the auditor underrelies on internal accounting control 22.__
and thereby increases substantive testing.
This is illustrated by situation

    A. I          B. II          C. III          D. IV

23. Which of the following MOST likely constitutes a weakness in the internal accounting 23.__
control of an EDP system?
The

    A. control clerk establishes control over data received by the EDP department and reconciles control totals after processing

    B. application programmer identifies programs required by the systems design and flowcharts the logic of these programs

C. systems analyst reviews output and controls the distribution of output from the EDP department

D. accounts payable clerk prepares data for computer processing and enters the data into the computer

24. Which of the following is LEAST likely to be evidence the auditor examines to determine whether operations are in compliance with the internal accounting control system?

    24.____

A. Records documenting usage of EDP programs
B. Cancelled supporting documents
C. Confirmations of accounts receivable
D. Signatures on authorization forms

25. The PRIMARY purpose of a management advisory services engagement is to help the client

    25.____

A. become more profitable by relying upon the CPA's existing personal knowledge about the client's business
B. improve the use of its capabilities and resources to achieve its objectives
C. document and quantify its future plans without impairing the CPA's objectivity or allowing the CPA to assume the role of management
D. obtain benefits that are guaranteed implicitly by the CPA

26. When unable to obtain sufficient competent evidential matter to determine whether certain client acts are illegal, the auditor would MOST likely issue

    26.____

A. an unqualified opinion with a separate explanatory paragraph
B. either a qualified opinion or an adverse opinion
C. either a disclaimer or opinion or a qualified opinion,
D. either an adverse opinion or a disclaimer of opinion

27. Which of the following statements BEST describes the auditor's responsibility regarding the detection of material errors and irregularities?

    27.____

A. The auditor is responsible for the failure to detect material errors and irregularities only when such failure results from the nonapplication of generally accepted accounting principles.
B. Extended auditing procedures are required to detect material errors and irregularities if the auditor's examination indicates that they may exist.
C. The auditor is responsible for the failure to detect material errors and irregularities only when the auditor fails to confirm receivables or observe inventories.
D. Extended auditing procedures are required to detect unrecorded transactions even if there is no evidence that material errors and irregularities may exist.

28. An abnormal fluctuation in gross profit that might suggest the need for extended audit procedures for sales and inventories would MOST likely be identified in the planning phase of the audit by the use of

    28.____

A. tests of transactions and balances
B. a preliminary review of internal accounting control
C. specialized audit programs
D. analytical review procedures

29. When considering internal control, an auditor should be aware of the concept of reasonable assurance, which recognizes that the   29.__

    A. segregation of incompatible functions is necessary to ascertain that internal control is effective
    B. employment of competent personnel provides assurance that the objectives of internal control will be achieved
    C. establishment and maintenance of a system of internal control is an important responsibility of the management and not of the auditor
    D. cost of internal control should not exceed the benefits expected to be derived from internal control

30. When performing an audit of a city that is subject to the requirements of the Uniform Single Audit Act of 1984, an auditor should adhere to   30.__

    A. Governmental Accounting Standards Board GENERAL STANDARDS
    B. Governmental Finance Officers Association GOVERNMENTAL ACCOUNTING, AUDITING, AND FINANCIAL REPORTING PRINCIPLES
    C. General Accounting Office STANDARDS FOR AUDIT OF GOVERNMENTAL ORGANIZATIONS, PROGRAMS, ACTIVITIES, AND FUNCTIONS
    D. Securities and Exchange Commission REGULATION S-X

———

# KEY (CORRECT ANSWERS)

| | | | | |
|---|---|---|---|---|
| 1. | D | | 16. | D |
| 2. | B | | 17. | B |
| 3. | A | | 18. | B |
| 4. | C | | 19. | C |
| 5. | D | | 20. | D |
| 6. | C | | 21. | B |
| 7. | B | | 22. | C |
| 8. | D | | 23. | C |
| 9. | D | | 24. | C |
| 10. | D | | 25. | B |
| 11. | C | | 26. | C |
| 12. | C | | 27. | B |
| 13. | C | | 28. | D |
| 14. | B | | 29. | D |
| 15. | A | | 30. | C |

———

# EXAMINATION SECTION
## TEST 1

DIRECTIONS: Each question or incomplete statement is followed by several suggested answers or completions. Select the one that BEST answers the question or completes the Statement. *PRINT THE LETTER OF THE CORRECT ANSWER IN THE SPACE AT THE RIGHT.*

1. Gross income of an individual for Federal income tax purposes does NOT include          1.____

    A. interest credited to a bank savings account
    B. gain from the sale of sewer authority bonds
    C. back pay received as a result of job reinstatement
    D. interest received from State Dormitory Authority bonds

2. A cash-basis, calendar-year taxpayer purchased an annuity policy at a total cost of          2.____
$20,000. Starting on January 1 of 2006, he began to receive annual payments of $1,500.
His life expectancy as of that date was 16 years.
The amount of annuity income to be included in his gross income for the taxable year
2006 is

    A. none        B. $250        C. $1,250        D. $1,500

3. The transactions related to a municipal police retirement system should be included in          3.____
a(n)

    A. intra-governmental service fund
    B. trust fund
    C. general fund
    D. special revenue fund

4. The budget for a given cost during a given period was $100,000. The actual cost for the          4.____
period was $90,000. Based upon these facts, one should say that the responsible man-
ager has done a better than expected job in controlling the cost if the cost is

    A. variable and actual production equaled budgeted production
    B. a discretionary fixed cost and actual production equaled budgeted production
    C. variable and actual production was 90% of budgeted production
    D. variable and actual production was 80% of budgeted production

5. In the conduct of an audit, the *most practical* method by which an accountant can satisfy          5.____
himself as to the physical existence of inventory is to

    A. be present and observe personally the audited firm's physical inventory being
taken
    B. independently verify an adequate proportion of all inventory operations performed
by the audited firm
    C. mail confirmation requests to vendors of merchandise sold to the audited firm
within the inventory year
    D. review beforehand the adequacy of the audited firm's plan for inventory taking, and
during the actual inventory-taking stages, verify that this plan is being followed

Questions 6-7.

DIRECTIONS:   The following information applies to Questions 6 and 7.

For the month of March, the ABC Manufacturing Corporation's estimated factory overhead for an expected volume of 15,000 lbs. of a product was as follows:

|  | Amount | Overhead Rate Per Unit |
|---|---|---|
| Fixed Overhead | $3,000 | $.20 |
| Variable Overhead | $9,000 | $.60 |

Actual volume was 10,000 lbs. and actual overhead expense was $7,700.

6.  The Spending (Budget) Variance was                                6._

    A.  $1,300 (Favorable)          B.  $6,000 (Favorable)
    C.  $7,700 (Favorable)          D.  $9,000 (Favorable)

7.  The Idle Capacity Variance was                                    7._

    A.  $300 (Favorable)          B.  $1,000 (Unfavorable)
    C.  $1,300 (Favorable)          D.  $8,000 (Unfavorable)

Questions 8-11.

DIRECTIONS:   Answer Questions 8 through 11 on the basis of the information given below.

A bookkeeper, who was not familiar with proper accounting procedures, prepared the following financial report for Largor Corporation as of December 31, 2006. In addition to the
errors in presentation, additional data below was not considered in the preparation of the
report. Restate this balance sheet in proper form, giving recognition to the additional data, so
that you will be able to determine the required information to answer Questions 8 through 11.

LARGOR CORPORATION
December 31, 2006

Current Assets
| Cash |  | $110,000 |  |
|---|---|---|---|
| Marketable Securities |  | 53,000 |  |
| Accounts Receivable | $261,400 |  |  |
| Accounts Payable | 125,000 | 136,400 |  |
| Inventories |  | 274,000 |  |
| Prepaid Expenses |  | 24,000 |  |
| Treasury Stock |  | 20,000 |  |
| Cash Surrender Value of |  |  |  |
|   Officers' Life Insuranc Policies |  | 105,000 | $722 , 400 |

Plant Assets
| Equipment |  | 350,000 |  |
|---|---|---|---|
| Building | 200,000 |  |  |
|   Reserve for Plant |  |  |  |
|   Expansion | 75,000 | 125,000 |  |
| Land |  | 47,500 | 522,500 |
|   TOTAL ASSETS |  |  | $1,244,900 |

Liabilities

| | | | |
|---|---|---|---|
| Salaries Payable | | 16,500 | |
| Cash Dividend Payable | | 50,000 | |
| Stock Dividend Payable | | 70,000 | |
| Bonds Payable | 200,000 | | |
| Less Sinking Fund | 90,000 | 110,000 | |
| TOTAL LIABILITIES | | | $246,500 |

Stockholders' Equity:

Paid In Capital

| | | |
|---|---|---|
| Common Stock | | 350,000 |

Retained Earnings and Reserves

| | | | |
|---|---|---|---|
| Reserve for Income Taxes | 90,000 | | |
| Reserve for Doubtful Accounts | 6,500 | | |
| Reserve for Treasury Stock | 20,000 | | |
| Reserve for Depreciation Equipment | 70,000 | | |
| Reserve for Depreciation Building | 80,000 | | |
| Premium on Common stock | 15,000 | | |
| Retained Earnings | 366,900 | 648,400 | 998.400 |

TOTAL LIABILITIES & EQUITY $1,244,900

Additional Data

A. Bond Payable will mature eight (8) years from Balance Sheet date.

B. The Stock Dividend Payable was declared on December 31, 2006.

C. The Reserve for Income Taxes represents the balance due on the estimated liability for taxes on income for the year ended December 31.

D. Advances from Customers at the Balance Sheet date totaled $13,600. This total is still credited against Accounts Receivable.

E. Prepaid Expenses include Unamortized Mortgage Costs of $15,000.

F. Marketable Securities were recorded at cost. Their market value at December 31, 2006 was $50,800.

8. After restatement of the balance sheet in proper form and giving recognition to the additional data, the Total Current Assets should be

    A. $597,400     B. $702,400     C. $712,300     D. $827,300

8._____

9. After restatement of the balance sheet in proper form and giving recognition to the additional data, the Total Current Liabilities should be

    A. $261,500     B. $281,500     C. $295,100     D. . D. $370,100

9._____

10. After restatement of the balance sheet in proper form and giving recognition to the additional data, the net book value of plant and equipment should be

    A. $400,000     B. B, $447,500     C. $550,000     D. $597,500

10._____

11. After restatement of the balance sheet in proper form and giving recognition to the additional data, the Stockholders Equity should be

    A. $320,000     B. $335,000     C. $764,700     D. $874,700

11._____

12. When preparing the financial statement, dividends in arrears on preferred stock should be treated as a    12.__

    A.   contingent liability               B.   deduction from capital
    C.   parenthetical remark           D.   valuation reserve

13. The IPC Corporation has an intangible asset which it values at $1,000,000 and has a life expectancy of 60 years. The *appropriate* span of write-off, as determined by good accounting practice, should be _____ years.    13.__

    A.  17           B.  34           C.  40           D.  60

14. The following information was used in costing inventory on October 31:    14.__

| October | 1 - | Beginning inventory - | 800 units | @ $1.20 |
|---|---|---|---|---|
| | 4 - | Received | 200 units | @ $1.40 |
| | 16 - | Issued | 400 units | |
| | 24 - | Received | 200 units | @ $1.60 |
| | 27 - | Issued | 500 units | |

Using the LIFO method of inventory evaluation (end-of-month method), the total dollar value of the inventory at October 31 was    14.__

    A.  $360         B.  $460         C.  $600         D.  $1,200

15. If a $400,000 par value bond issue paying 8%, with interest dates of June 30 and December 31, is sold in November 1 for par plus accrued interest, the cash proceeds received by the issuer on November 1 should be *approximately*    15.__

    A.  $405,000       B.  $408,000       C.  $411,000       D.  $416,000

16. The TOTAL interest cost to the issuer of a bond issue sold for more than its face value is the periodic interest payment    16.__

    A.  *plus* the discount amortization
    B.  *plus* the premium amortization
    C.  *minus* the discount amortization
    D.  *minus* the premium amortization

17. If shareholders donate shares of stock back to the company, such stock received by the company is *properly* classified as    17.__

    A.  Treasury stock
    B.  Unissued stock
    C.  Other assets - investment
    D.  Current assets - investment

18. Assume the following transactions have occurred:    18.__
    1.  10,000 shares of capital stock of Omer Corp., par value $50, have been sold and issued on initial sale @ $55 per share during the month of June
    2.  2,000 shares of previously issued stock were purchased from shareholders during the month of September @ $58 per share.

As of September 30, the stockholders' equity section TOTAL should be

    A.  $434,000       B.  $450,000       C.  $480,000       D.  $550,000

19. Mr. Diak, a calendar-year taxpayer in the construction business, agrees to construct a     19._____
    building for the Supermat Corporation to cost a total of $500,000 and to require about
    two years to complete. By December 31, 2005, he has expended $150,000 in costs, and
    it was determined that the building was 35% completed.
    If Mr. Diak is reporting income under the completed contract method, the amount of
    gross income he will report for 2005 is

    A.  none            B.  $25,000            C.  $175,000            D.  $350,000

20. When the Board of Directors of a firm uses the present-value technique to aid in deciding     20._____
    whether or not to buy a new plant asset, it needs to have information reflecting

    A.  the cost of the new asset only
    B.  the increased production from use of new asset only
    C.  an estimated rate of return
    D.  the book value of the asset

———

# KEY (CORRECT ANSWERS)

| | | | |
|---|---|---|---|
| 1. | D | 11. | D |
| 2. | B | 12. | C |
| 3. | B | 13. | C |
| 4. | A | 14. | A |
| 5. | D | 15. | C |
| 6. | A | 16. | D |
| 7. | B | 17. | A |
| 8. | C | 18. | A |
| 9. | C | 19. | A |
| 10. | B | 20. | C |

———

# TEST 2

DIRECTIONS:  Each question or incomplete statement is followed by several suggested answers or completions. Select the one that BEST answers the question or completes the statement. *PRINT THE LETTER OF THE CORRECT ANSWER IN THE SPACE AT THE RIGHT.*

Questions 1-3.

DIRECTIONS:  The following information applies to Questions 1 through 3.

During your audit of the Avon Company, you find the following errors in the records of the company:

1.  Incorrect exclusion from the final inventory of items costing $3,000 for which the purchase was not recorded.
2.  Inclusion in the final inventory of goods costing $5,000, although a purchase was not recorded. The goods in question were being held on consignment from Re1drey Company.
3.  Incorrect exclusion of $2,000 from the inventory count at the end of the period. The goods were in transit (F.O.B. shipping point); the invoice had been received and the purchase recorded.
4.  Inclusion of items on the receiving dock that were being held for return to the vendor because of damage. In counting the goods in the receiving department, these items were incorrectly included. With respect to these goods, a purchase of $4,000 had been recorded.

The records (uncorrected) showed the following amounts:
1.  Purchases, $170,000
2.  Pretax income, $15,000
3.  Accounts payable, $20,000; and
4.  Inventory at the end of the period, $40,000.

1.  The *corrected* inventory is                                                                      1._

    A.  $36,000        B.  $42,000        C.  $43,000        D.  $44,000

2.  The *corrected* income for the year is                                                          2._

    A.  $12,000        B.  $15,000        C.  $17,000        D.  $18,000

3.  The *correct* accounts payable liabilities are                                                3._

    A.  $16,000        B.  $17,000        C.  $19,000        D.  $23,000

4.  An auditing procedure that is *most likely* to reveal the existence of a contingent liability is   4._

    A.  a review of vouchers paid during the month following the year end
    B.  confirmation of accounts payable
    C.  an inquiry directed to legal counsel
    D.  confirmation of mortgage notes

Questions 5-6.

DIRECTIONS:   The following information is to be used in answering Questions 5 and 6.

Mr. Zelev operates a business as a sole proprietor and uses the cash basis for reporting income for income tax purposes. His bank account during 2006 for the business shows receipts totaling $285,000 and cash payments totaling $240,000. Included in the cash payments were payments for three-year business insurance policies whose premiums totaled $1,575. It was determined that the expired premiums for this year were $475. Further examination of the accounts and discussion with Mr. Zelev revealed the fact that included in the receipts were the following items, as well as the proceeds received from customers:

$15,000 which Mr. Zelev took from his savings account and deposited in the business account.

$20,000 which Mr. Zelev received from the bank as a loan which will be repaid next year.

Included in the cash payments were $10,000 which Mr. Zelev took on a weekly basis from the business receipts to use for his personal expenses.

5.   The amount of net income to be reported for income tax purposes for calendar year 2006 for Mr. Zelev is

5.____

   A.  $21,100          B.  $26,100          C.  $31,100          D.  $46,100

6.   Assuming the same facts as those reported above, Mr. Zelev would be required to pay a self-employment tax for 2006 of

6.____

   A.  $895.05          B.  $1,208.70          C.  $1,234.35          D.  $1,666.90

7.   For the year ended December 31, 2006, you are given the following information relative to the income and expense statements for the Sungam Manufacturers, Inc.:

7.____

Sales ..................................................................................................$1,000,000
   Sales Returns ..................................................................................95,000

Cost of Sales
Opening Inventories                    $200,000
Purchases During the Year              567,000
Direct Labor Costs                     240,000
Factory Overhead                        24,400
Inventories End of Year                235,000

On June 15, 2006, a fire destroyed the plant and all of the inventories then on hand. You are given the following information and asked to ascertain the amount of the estimated inventory loss.

Sales up to June 15                    $545,000
Purchased to June 15                    254,500
Direct Labor                            233,000
Overhead                                 14,550
Salvaged Inventory                       95,000
The *estimated* inventory loss is

   A.  $95,000          B.  $162,450          C.  $189,450          D.  $257,450

8. Losses and excessive costs with regard to inventory can occur in any one of several operating functions of an organization.
The operating function which bears the GREATEST responsibility for the failure to give proper consideration to transportation costs of material acquisitions is

    A. accounting                      B. purchasing
    C. receiving                       D. shipping

8.\_

Question's 9-17.

DIRECTIONS: Questions 9 through 17 are to be answered on the basis of the information given below.

You are conducting an audit of the PAP Company, which has a contract to supply the municipal hospitals with specialty refrigerators on a cost-plus basis. The following information is available:

| | |
|---|---|
| Materials purchased | $1,946,700 |

Inventories, January 1

| | |
|---|---|
| Materials | 268,000 |
| Finished Goods (100 units) | 43,000 |
| Direct Labor | 2,125,800 |
| Factory Overhead (40% variable) | 764,000 |
| Marketing Expenses (all fixed) | 516,000 |
| Administrative Expenses (all fixed) | 461,000 |
| Sales (12,400 units) | 6,634,000 |

Inventories, March 31

| | |
|---|---|
| Materials | 167,000 |
| Finished Goods (200 units) | (omitted) |
| No Work In Process | |

9. The *net income* for the period is

    A. $755,500                     B. $1,237,500
    C. $1,732,500               D. $4,980,500

9.\_

10. The *number* of units manufactured is

    A. 12,400       B. 12,500       C. 12,600       D. 12,700

10.\_

11. The *unit cost* of refrigerators manufactured is *most nearly*

    A. $389.00       B. $395.00       C. $398.00       D. $400.00

11.\_

12. The *total* variable costs are

    A. $305,600                   B. $764,000
    C. $4,479,100              D. $4,937,500

12.\_

13. The *total* fixed costs are

    A. $458,400                   B. $1,435,400
    C. $1,471,800              D. $1,741,000

13.\_

While you are conducting your audit, the PAP Company advises you that they have changed their inventory costing from FIFO to LIFO. You are interested in pursuing the matter further because this change will affect the cost of the refrigerators. An examination of material part 2-317 inventory card shows the following activity:

May 2 - Received 100 units @ $5.40 per unit
May 8 - Received 30 units @ $8.00 per unit
May 15 - Issued 50 units
May 22 - Received 120 units @ $9.00 per unit
May 29 - Issued 100 units

14. Using the FIFO method under a perpetual inventory control system, the *total* cost of the units issued in May is   14.____

   A. $690      B. $960      C. $1,590      D. $1,860

15. Using the FIFO method under a perpetual inventory control system, the *value* of the closing inventory is   15.____

   A. $780      B. $900      C. $1,080      D. $1,590

16. Using the LIFO method under a perpetual inventory control system, the *total* cost of the units issued in May is   16.____

   A. $1,248      B. $1,428      C. $1,720      D. $1,860

17. Using the LIFO method under a perpetual inventory control system, the *value* of the closing inventory is   17.____

   A. $612      B. $780      C. $1,512      D. $1,680

Questions 18-20.

DIRECTIONS: For Questions 18 through 20, consider that the EEF Corporation has a fully integrated cost accounting system.

18. Unit cost of manufacturing dresses was $7.00. Spoiled dresses numbered 400 with a sales value of $800. When it is not customary to have a Spoiled Work account, the *most appropriate* account to be credited is   18.____

   A. Work In Process      B. Cost of Sales
   C. Manufacturing Overhead      D. Finished Goods

19. Overtime premium for factory workers (direct labor) totaled $400 for the payroll period. This was due to inadequate plant capacity. The account to be *debited* is   19.____

   A. Work In Process      B. Cost of Sales
   C. Manufacturing Overhead      D. Finished Goods

20. A month-end physical inventory of stores shows a shortage of $175. The account to be *debited* to correct this shortage is   20.____

   A. Stores      B. Work In Process
   C. Cost of Sales      D. Manufacturing Overhead

# KEY (CORRECT ANSWERS)

| | | | |
|---|---|---|---|
| 1. | A | 11. | B |
| 2. | A | 12. | C |
| 3. | C | 13. | B |
| 4. | C | 14. | B |
| 5. | A | 15. | B |
| 6. | D | 16. | A |
| 7. | B | 17. | A |
| 8. | B | 18. | A |
| 9. | A | 19. | C |
| 10. | B | 20. | C |

# EXAMINATION SECTION
## TEST 1

DIRECTIONS:   Each question or incomplete statement is followed by several suggested answers or completions. Select the one that BEST answers the question or completes the statement. *PRINT THE LETTER OF THE CORRECT ANSWER IN THE SPACE AT THE RIGHT.*

1.  The Donaldson Company's cash balance includes a sum of $1,200,000 appropriated by the Board of Directors for the purchase of new equipment.
    On its financial statements, this amount should be included on the     1.____

    A.  balance sheet as a current asset
    B.  balance sheet as a non-current asset, specifically identified
    C.  balance sheet as a fixed asset, included as part of plant cost
    D.  income statement as a non-operating expense

2.  The trial balance of the Davis Corporation as of June 30, 2006, the end of its fiscal year, included opposite the title *Estimated Federal Income Taxes Accrued* the amount of $35,000, which included the company's estimate of the Federal income tax it would have to pay for its 2006 fiscal year and the amount of an unpaid additional assessment for the 2003 fiscal year.
    This amount should appear on the balance sheet as a(n)     2.____

    A.  general reserve
    B.  reduction of current assets
    C.  current liability
    D.  allocation of retained income

3.  A weekly payroll check was issued to an hourly employee based upon 88 hours of work instead of the normal 38 hours. The time card was somewhat illegible, and the number looked like it could have been 88.
    The BEST control procedure to prevent such an error would be     3.____

    A.  desk checking             B.   a hash total
    C.  a limit test              D.   a code check

4.  In preparing a bank reconciliation, outstanding checks should be     4.____

    A.  *deducted* from the balance per books
    B.  *deducted* from the balance per bank statement
    C.  *added* to the balance per books
    D.  *added* to the balance per bank statement

5.  Independence is essential and is expected under the generally accepted auditing standards.
    The fact and appearance of integrity and objectivity are BEST maintained if     5.____

    A.  the auditor is unbiased
    B.  the auditor is aware of the problem of third party liability
    C.  there is no financial relationship between the client and the auditor
    D.  all financial relationships between the auditor and the client are reported in footnote form

6. An audit program is a plan of action and is used to guide the auditor in planning his work.   6.\_\_
   Such a program, if standardized, must be modified to

    A. observe limits that management places on the audit
    B. counteract internal control weaknesses
    C. meet the limited training of the auditor
    D. limit interference with work of the firm being audited

7. In auditing the *Owner's Equity* section of any company, the section related to a publicly-   7.\_\_
   held corporation which uses a transfer agent and registrar would be more intricate than
   the audit of a partnership.
   Therefore, the procedure that an auditor should use in this case is to

    A. obtain a listing of the number of shares of securities outstanding
    B. make a count of the number of shareholders
    C. determine that all stock transfers have been properly handled
    D. count the number of shares of stock in the treasury

8. In recent years, it has become increasingly more important to determine the correct   8.\_\_
   number of shares outstanding when auditing the owner's equity accounts.
   This is TRUE because

    A. there has been more fraud with respect to securities issued
    B. there are increased complexities determining the earnings per share
    C. there are more large corporations
    D. the auditor has to test the amount of invested capital

9. In auditing corporation records, an auditor must refer to some corporate documents that   9.\_\_
   are NOT accounting documents. The one of the following to which he is LEAST likely to
   refer is

    A. minutes of the board of directors meeting
    B. articles of incorporation of the corporation
    C. correspondence with public relations firms and the shareholders
    D. the by-laws of the corporation

10. A generally accepted auditing procedure which has been required by AICPA require-   10.\_\_
    ments is the observation of inventories.
    Since it is impossible to observe the entire inventory of a large firm, the auditor may
    satisfy this requirement by

    A. establishing the balance by the use of a gross profit percentage method
    B. using sampling procedures to verify the count made by the client
    C. accepting the perpetual inventory records, once he has established that the entries
       are arithmetically accurate
    D. accepting the management statement that the inventory is correct as to quantity
       where observation is difficult

11. Materiality is an important consideration in all aspects of an audit examination. Attention   11.\_\_
    must be given to accounts with small and zero balances when examining accounts pay-
    able.
    This does not conflict with the concept of materiality because

A.   the size of a balance is no clue to possible understatement of a liability
B.   the balance of the account is not a measure of materiality
C.   a sampling technique may suggest examining those accounts under consideration
D.   the total of the accounts payable may be a material amount and, therefore, no individual account payable should be eliminated from review

12.   In establishing the amount of a liability recorded on the books, which of the following types of evidence should an auditor consider to be the MOST reliable?

12._____

A.   A check issued by the company and bearing the payee's endorsement which is included with the bank statement
B.   Confirmation of an account payable balance mailed by and returned directly to the auditor
C.   A sales invoice issued by the client with a delivery receipt from an outside trucker attached
D.   A working paper prepared by the client's accountant and reviewed by the client's controller

13.   Prior period adjustments as defined by APB Opinion #9 issued by the AICPA never flow through the income statement.
The one of the following which is NOT one of the four criteria established by APB #9 for meeting the qualifications for treatment as a prior period adjustment is that the adjustment item

13._____

A.   is not susceptible to reasonable extension prior to the current period
B.   must be determined primarily by someone other than company management
C.   can be specifically identified with and directly related to the business activities of a particular prior period
D.   when placed in the current period would give undesirable results of operations

14.   The subject caption which does NOT belong in a report of a financial audit and review of operations of a public agency is

14._____

A.   Audit Program
B.   Description of Agency Organization and Function
C.   Summary Statement of Findings
D.   Details of Findings

15.   At the inception of an audit of a public assistance agency, you ascertain that the one-year period of your audit includes 240,000 serially numbered payment vouchers.
The sample selection which would enable you to render the MOST generally acceptable opinion on the number of ineligible persons receiving public assistance is

15._____

A.   the number of vouchers issued in a one-month period
B.   every hundredth voucher
C.   a random statistical selection
D.   an equal size block of vouchers from each month

16. Of the following, the one which BEST describes an internal control system is the    16.__

    A.   division of the handling and recording of each transaction into component parts so as to involve at least two persons, with each performing an unduplicated part of each transaction
    B.   expansion of the worksheet to include provisions for adjustments to the books of account prior to preparation of the financial statements
    C.   recording of transactions affecting negotiable instruments in accordance with the principles of debit and credit, and giving these instruments special treatment if they are interest or non-interest bearing notes
    D.   taking of discounts, when properly authorized by the vendor, as an incentive for prompt payment

17. During audits of small businesses, an accountant is less likely to find that these establishments have a system of internal control comparable to larger firms because small businesses GENERALLY    17.__

    A.   can absorb the cost of small fraudulent acts which may be perpetrated
    B.   benefit more than larger firms by prevention of fraud than by detection of fraud
    C.   have limited staff and the costs of maintaining the system are high
    D.   use a double entry system which serves as a substitute for internal control

18. In the performance of a financial audit, especially one where there is a need for a thorough knowledge of law, an accountant would BEST be advised to    18.__

    A.   rely on the testimony of witnesses, as they may be found during the course of the audit, in preference to the written record
    B.   rely on the presumption that the client's actions are illegal when the audit discloses meager facts or evidence
    C.   be aware of the specific legal objectives he is attempting to attain by means of his audit
    D.   be aware of different conclusions he can reach depending upon what facts are stressed or discounted in his audit

19. There are various types of budgets which are used to measure different government activities.
The type of budget which PARTICULARLY measures input of resource as compared with output of service is the _____ budget.    19.__

    A.   capital               B.   traditional
    C.   performance        D.   program

20. Bank balances are usually confirmed through the use of a standard bank confirmation form as authorized by the AICPA and the Bank Administration Institute.
In addition to bank balances, these confirmations ALSO confirm    20.__

    A.   the credit rating of the client
    B.   details of all deposits during the past month
    C.   loans and contingent liabilities outstanding
    D.   securities held by the bank as custodian for the client

# KEY (CORRECT ANSWERS)

| | | | | |
|---|---|---|---|---|
| 1. | B | | 11. | A |
| 2. | C | | 12. | B |
| 3. | C | | 13. | D |
| 4. | B | | 14. | A |
| 5. | C | | 15. | C |
| | | | | |
| 6. | B | | 16. | A |
| 7. | A | | 17. | C |
| 8. | B | | 18. | C |
| 9. | C | | 19. | C |
| 10. | B | | 20. | C |

———

# TEST 2

DIRECTIONS: Each question or incomplete statement is followed by several suggested answers or completions. Select the one that BEST answers the question or completes the statement. *PRINT THE LETTER OF THE CORRECT ANSWER IN THE SPACE AT THE RIGHT.*

Questions 1-3.

DIRECTIONS: Questions 1 through 3 are based on the classification of items into the appropriate section of a corporation balance sheet. The list of sections to be used is given below:

| | |
|---|---|
| Current assets | Investments |
| Current liabilities | Long-term liabilities |
| Deferred credits | Paid-in capital |
| Deferred expenses | Plant assets |
| Intangible assets | Retained earnings |

1. With respect to *Bonds Payable Due* in 2015, the PROPER classification is        1.__

    A.  Investments                B.  Paid-in capital
    C.  Retained earnings      D.  Long-term liabi

2. With respect to *Premium on Common Stock,* the PROPER classification is        2.__

    A.  Intangible assets       B.  Investments
    C.  Retained earnings      D.  Paid-in capital

3. With respect to *Organization Costs,* the PROPER classification is        3.__

    A.  Intangible assets       B.  Investments
    C.  Plant assets             D.  Current liabilities

4. J. Frost operates a small, individually owned repair service and maintains adequate dou-        4.__
ble entry records. A review of his bank accounts and other available financial records yields the following information:
Deposits made during 2005 per bank statements totalled $360,000. Deposits included a bank loan of $25,000 and an additional investment by Frost of $5,000. Disbursements during 2005 per bank statements totalled $305,000. This amount includes personal withdrawals of $28,500 and repayment of debt of $15,000.
The Net Equity of J. Frost at January 1, 2005 was determined to be $61,000.
Net Equity of J. Frost at December 31, 2005 was determined to be $67,000.
Based upon the *Net Worth* method, Frost's net income for the year ended December 31, 2005 was

    A.  $6,000        B.  $29,500       C.  $41,500       D.  $55,000

Questions 5-8.

DIRECTIONS: Questions 5 through 8 are based on the following Balance Sheet, Income Statement, and Notes relating to the books and records of the Hartman Corporation.

## BALANCE SHEET (000 omitted)

| | September 30, 2005 Debit | Credit | September 30, 2006 Debit | Credit |
|---|---|---|---|---|
| Cash | $ 18 | | $ 31 | |
| Accounts receivable | 28 | | 26 | |
| Inventory | 10 | | 15 | |
| Land | 40 | | 81 | |
| Building and equipment (Net) | 60 | | 65 | |
| Accounts payable | | $ 10 | | $ 11 |
| Notes payable - short-term | | 2 | | 2 |
| Bonds payable | | 50 | | 50 |
| Mortgage payable | | 20 | | 46 |
| Common stock | | 50 | | 86 |
| Retained earnings | | 24 | | 23 |
| | $156 | $156 | $218 | $218 |

### INCOME STATEMENT FOR FISCAL YEAR ENDING SEPTEMBER 30, 2006

Income :
Sales     $85
Cost of sales     40
Gross margin     $45

Expenses :
Depreciation     $ 5
Loss on sale of fixed assets     2
Other operating expenses     32
Total expenses     $39
Net income     $ 6

NOTES:
1. Dividend declared during the year 2006, $7,000.
2. Acquired land; gave $36,000 common stock and cash for the balance.
3. Wrote off $1,000 accounts receivable as uncollectible.
4. Acquired equipment; gave note secured by mortgage of $26,000.
5. Sold equipment; net cost per books, $16,000, sales price $14,000.

5. The amount of funds provided from net income for the year ended September 30, 2006 is    5.____

   A. $6,000     B. $7,000     C. $13,000     D. $14,000

6. Financing and investing activities not affecting working capital are reported under the    6.____
rules of APB #19. Notes 1 through 5 refer to various transactions on the books of the
Hartman Corporation.
Select the answer which refers to the numbers reflecting the concept mentioned here.

A. Notes 1, 3, and 5     B. Notes 2 and 4
C. Notes 2, 4, and 5     D. All five notes

7. Funds applied for the acquisition of the land are        7.___

 A. $5,000   B. $36,000   C. $41,000   D. None

8. The net change in working capital from 2005 to 2006 is     8.___

 A. $6,000   B. $16,000   C. $22,000   D. $35,000

9. Sales during July 2005 for the Magnum Corporation, operating in Los Angeles, were 9.___
$378,000, of which $150,000 were on account. The sales figures given include the total
sales tax charged to retail customers. (Assume a sales tax rate on all sales of 8%.)
The CORRECT sales tax liability for July 2005 should be shown as

 A. $3,024   B. $18,240   C. $28,000   D. $30,240

10. Of the following statement ratios, the one that BEST represents a measure of cost effi- 10.___
ciency is

 A. Acid Test Ratio
 B. Operating Costs to Net Sales Ratio
 C. Cost of Manufacturing to Plant Assets ratio
 D. Earnings Per Share

Questions 11-13.

DIRECTIONS: Answer Questions 11 through 13 on the basis of the following information.

 An examination of the books and records of the Kay May Corporation, a machinery
wholesaler, reveals the following facts for the year ended December 31, 2005:

 a. Merchandise was sold and billed F.O.B. shipping point on December 31, 2005 at a
sales price of $7,500. Although the merchandise costing $6,000 was ready for shipment on that date, the trucking company did not call for the merchandise until January
2, 2006. It was not included in the inventory count taken on December 31, 2005.
 b. Merchandise with a sales price of $5,500 was billed and shipped to the customer on
December 31, 2005. The merchandise costing $4,800 was not included in the inven-
tory count taken on that day. Terms of sale were F.O.B. destination.
 c. Merchandise costing $5,000 was recorded as a purchase on December 26, 2005.
The merchandise was not included in the inventory count taken on December 31,
2005 since, upon examination, it was found to be defective and was in the process of
being returned to the vendor.
 d. Merchandise costing $2,500 was received on December 31, 2005. It was included in
the inventory count on that date. Although the invoice was dated January 3, 2006, the
purchase was recorded in the December 2005 Purchases Journal.
 e. Merchandise costing $4,000 was received on January 3, 2006. It was shipped F.O.B.
destination, and the invoice was dated December 30, 2005. The invoice was recorded
in the December 2005 Purchases Journal, and the merchandise was included in the
December 31, 2005 inventory.

11. The net change to correct the inventory value as of December 31, 2005 is:　　11.____

    A. *Increase $800*　　　　　　　　　B. *Increase $5,800*
    C. *Increase $6,800*　　　　　　　　　D. *Decrease $12,055*

12. The net change to correct the sales figure for the year 2005 is:　　12.____

    A. *Increase $2,000*　　　　　　　　　B. *Decrease $5,500*
    C. *Decrease $7,500*　　　　　　　　　D. *Decrease $13,000*

13. The net change to correct the purchases figure for the year 2005 is:　　13.____

    A. *Decrease $11,500*　　　　　　　　B. *Decrease $4,000*
    C. *Decrease $5,000*　　　　　　　　　D. *Decrease $9,000*

Questions 14-18.

DIRECTIONS:　Each of the following Questions 14 through 18 consists of a description of a transaction that indicates a two-fold effect on the Balance Sheet. Each of these transactions may be classified under one of the following categories:

    A. Assets are Understated, Retained Earnings are Understated
    B. Assets are Overstated, Retained Earnings are Overstated
    C. Liabilities are Understated, Retained Earnings are Overstated
    D. Liabilities are Overstated, Retained Earnings are Understated

    Examine each question carefully. In the correspondingly numbered space at the right, print the letter preceding the category above which BEST describes the effect of each transaction on the Balance Sheet as of December 31, 2005.

14. A major equipment purchase was made at the beginning of 2005. The equipment had an estimated six-year useful life, and depreciation was overlooked at December 31, 2005.　　14.____

15. Unearned Rental Income was properly credited when received early in the year. No year-end adjustment was made to transfer the earned portion to an appropriate account.　　15.____

16. Goods on hand at a branch office were excluded from the year-end physical inventory. The purchase of these goods had been properly recorded.　　16.____

17. Accrued Interest on Notes Receivable was overlooked as of December 31, 2005.　　17.____

18. Accrued Federal Income Taxes for 2005 have never been recorded.　　18.____

19. The following are account balances for the dates shown:　　19.____

| | Dec. 31, 2006 | Dec. 31, 2005 |
|---|---|---|
| Current Assets : | | |
| Cash | $168,000 | $ 60,000 |
| Short-term investments | 16,000 | 20,000 |
| Accounts receivable (net) | 160,000 | 100,000 |
| Inventory | 60,000 | 40,000 |
| Prepaid expenses | 4,000 | 0 |

Current Liabilities:

| | | |
|---|---|---|
| Accounts payable | 110,000 | 80,000 |
| Dividends payable | 30,000 | 0 |

Given the above account balances, the CHANGE in working capital is a(n)

A.  *increase* of $128,000  
B.  *decrease* of $128,000  
C.  *increase* of $188,000  
D.  *decrease* of $188,000

20.  In conducting an audit of plant assets, which of the following accounts MUST be exam-    20.___
ined in order to ascertain that additions to plant assets have been correctly stated and
reflect charges that are properly capitalized?

A.  Accounts receivable  
B.  Sales income  
C.  Maintenance and repairs  
D.  Investments

-------

# KEY (CORRECT ANSWERS)

| | | | |
|---|---|---|---|
| 1. | D | 11. | A |
| 2. | D | 12. | B |
| 3. | A | 13. | D |
| 4. | B | 14. | B |
| 5. | C | 15. | D |
| 6. | B | 16. | A |
| 7. | A | 17. | A |
| 8. | B | 18. | C |
| 9. | C | 19. | A |
| 10. | B | 20. | C |

-------

# INTERPRETING STATISTICAL DATA
## GRAPHS, CHARTS AND TABLES
# EXAMINATION SECTION
# TEST 1

DIRECTIONS:    Each question or incomplete statement is followed by several suggested answers or completions. Select the one that BEST answers the question or completes the statement. *PRINT THE LETTER OF THE CORRECT ANSWER IN THE SPACE AT THE RIGHT.*

Questions 1-3.

DIRECTIONS:    Questions 1 through 3 are to be answered SOLELY on the basis of the following table.

QUARTERLY SALES REPORTED BY MAJOR INDUSTRY GROUPS

DECEMBER 2007 - FEBRUARY 2009

Reported Sales, Taxable & Non-Taxable
(In Millions)

| Industry Groups | 12/07-2/08 | 3/08-5/08 | 6/08-8/08 | 9/08-11/08 | 12/08-2/09 |
|---|---|---|---|---|---|
| Retailers | 2,802 | 2,711 | 2,475 | 2,793 | 2,974 |
| Wholesalers | 2,404 | 2,237 | 2,269 | 2,485 | 2,512 |
| Manufacturers | 3,016 | 2,888 | 3,001 | 3,518 | 3,293 |
| Services | 1,034 | 1,065 | 984 | 1,132 | 1,092 |

1.   The trend in total reported sales may be described as    1._____

    A.  downward         B.  downward and upward
    C.  horizontal        D.  upward

2.   The two industry groups that reveal a similar seasonal pattern for the period December 2007 through November 2008 are    2._____

    A.  retailers and manufacturers
    B.  retailers and wholesalers
    C.  wholesalers and manufacturers
    D.  wholesalers and service

3.   Reported sales were at a MINIMUM between    3._____

    A.  December 2007 and February 2008
    B.  March 2008 and May 2008
    C.  June 2008 and August 2008
    D.  September 2008 and November 2008

# TEST 2

DIRECTIONS: Each question or incomplete statement is followed by several suggested answers or completions. Select the one that BEST answers the question or completes the statement. *PRINT THE LETTER OF THE CORRECT ANSWER IN THE SPACE AT THE RIGHT.*

Questions 1-4.

DIRECTIONS: Questions 1 through 4 are to be answered SOLELY on the basis of the following information.

The income elasticity of demand for selected items of consumer demand in the United States are:

| Item | Elasticity |
|------|-----------|
| Airline Travel | 5.66 |
| Alcohol | .62 |
| Dentist Fees | 1.00 |
| Electric Utilities | 3.00 |
| Gasoline | 1.29 |
| Intercity Bus | 1.89 |
| Local Bus | 1.41 |
| Restaurant Meals | .75 |

1. The demand for the item listed below that would be MOST adversely affected by a decrease in income is

   A. alcohol
   C. gasoline
   B. electric utilities
   D. restaurant meals

1

2. The item whose relative change in demand would be the same as the relative change in income would be

   A. dentist fees
   C. restaurant meals
   B. gasoline
   D. none of the above

2

3. If income increases by 12 percent, the demand for restaurant meals may be expected to increase by

   A. 9 percent
   C. 16 percent
   B. 12 percent
   D. none of the above

3

4. On the basis of the above information, the item whose demand would be MOST adversely affected by an increase in the sales tax from 7 percent to 8 percent to be passed on to the consumer in the form of higher prices

   A. would be airline travel
   C. would be gasoline
   B. would be alcohol
   D. cannot be determined

4

———

# TEST 3

DIRECTIONS: Each question or incomplete statement is followed by several suggested answers or completions. Select the one that BEST answers the question or completes the statement. *PRINT THE LETTER OF THE CORRECT ANSWER IN THE SPACE AT THE RIGHT.*

Questions 1-3.

DIRECTIONS: Questions 1 through 3 are to be answered SOLELY on the basis of the following graphs depicting various relationships in a single retail store.

## GRAPH I
## RELATIONSHIP BETWEEN NUMBER OF CUSTOMERS
## STORE AND TIME OF DAY

**NO. OF CUSTOMERS**

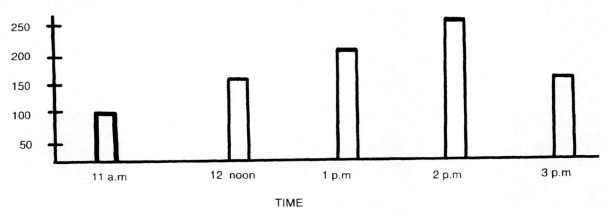

TIME

## GRAPH II
## RELATIONSHIP BETWEEN NUMBER OF CHECK-OUT LANES AVAILABLE
## IN STORE AND WAIT TIME FOR CHECK-OUT

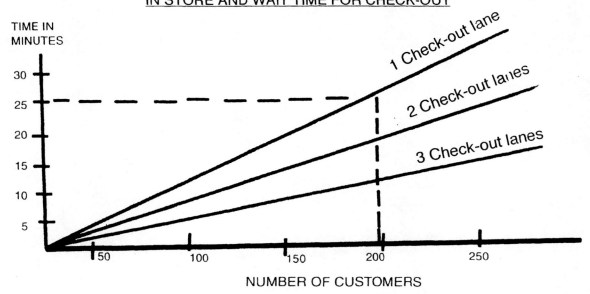

NUMBER OF CUSTOMERS

Note the dotted lines in Graph II. They demonstrate that, if there are 200 people in the store and only 1 check-out lane is open, the wait time will be 25 minutes.

1. At what time would a person be most likely NOT to have to wait more than 15 minutes if only one check-out lane is open?

   A.   11 A.M.          B.   12 Noon          C.   1 P.M.          D.   3 P.M.

2. At what time of day would a person have to wait the LONGEST to check out if 3 check-out lanes are available?

   A.   11 A.M.          B.   12 Noon          C.   1 P.M.          D.   2 P.M.

3. The difference in wait times between 1 and 3 check-out lanes at 3 P.M. is MOST NEARLY

   A.   5          B.   10          C.   15          D.   20

———

# TEST 4

DIRECTIONS: Each question or incomplete statement is followed by several suggested answers or completions. Select the one that BEST answers the question or completes the statement. *PRINT THE LETTER OF THE CORRECT ANSWER IN THE SPACE AT THE RIGHT.*

Questions 1-4.

DIRECTIONS: Questions 1 through 4 are to be answered SOLELY on the basis of the graph below.

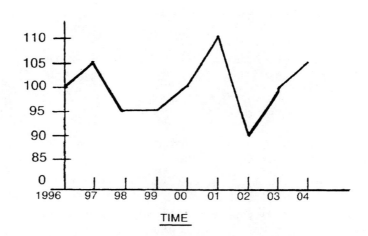

1.  Of the following, during what four-year period did the average output of computer opera-    1._____
    tors fall BELOW 100 sheets per hour?

    A.  1997-00          B.  1998-01          C.  2000-03          D.  2001-04

2.  The average percentage change in output over the previous year's output for the years    2._____
    1999 to 2002 is MOST NEARLY

    A.  2               B.  0               C.  -5              D.  -7

3.  The difference between the actual output for 2002 and the projected figure based upon    3._____
    the average increase from 1996-2001 is MOST NEARLY

    A.  18              B.  20              C.  22              D.  24

4.  Assume that after constructing the above graph you, an analyst, discovered that the    4._____
    average number of entries per sheet in 2002 was 25 (instead of 20) because of the com-
    plex nature of the work performed during that period.
    The average output in cards per hour for the period 2000-03, expressed in terms of 20
    items per sheet, would then be MOST NEARLY

    A.  95              B.  100             C.  105             D.  110

# TEST 5

DIRECTIONS: Each question or incomplete statement is followed by several suggested answers or completions. Select the one that BEST answers the question or completes the statement. *PRINT THE LETTER OF THE CORRECT ANSWER IN THE SPACE AT THE RIGHT.*

Questions 1-3.

DIRECTIONS: Questions 1 through 3 are to be answered on the basis of the following data assembled for a cost-benefit analysis.

|  | Cost | Benefit |
|---|---|---|
| No program | 0 | 0 |
| Alternative W | $ 3,000 | $ 6,000 |
| Alternative X | $10,000 | $17,000 |
| Alternative Y | $17,000 | $25,000 |
| Alternative Z | $30,000 | $32,000 |

1. From the point of view of selecting the alternative with the best cost benefit ratio, the BEST alternative is Alternative

    A. W          B. X          C. Y          D. Z

1.

2. From the point of view of selecting the alternative with the best measure of net benefit, the BEST alternative is Alternative

    A. W          B. X          C. Y          D. Z

2.

3. From the point of view of pushing public expenditure to the point where marginal benefit equals or exceeds marginal cost, the BEST alternative is Alternative

    A. W          B. X          C. Y          D. Z

3.

———

# TEST 6

DIRECTIONS: Each question or incomplete statement is followed by several suggested answers or completions. Select the one that BEST answers the question or completes the statement. *PRINT THE LETTER OF THE CORRECT ANSWER IN THE SPACE AT THE RIGHT.*

Questions 1-3.

DIRECTIONS: Questions 1 through 3 are to be answered SOLELY on the basis of the following data.

A series of cost-benefit studies of various alternative health programs yields the following results:

| Program | Benefit | Cost |
|---------|---------|------|
| K | 30 | 15 |
| L | 60 | 60 |
| M | 300 | 150 |
| N | 600 | 500 |

In answering Questions 1 and 2, assume that all programs can be increased or decreased in scale without affecting their individual benefit-to-cost ratios.

1. The benefit-to-cost ratio of Program M is                                                                              1.____

   A.  10:1          B.  5:1          C.  2:1          D.  1:2

2. The budget ceiling for one or more of the programs included in the study is set at 75         2.____
   units.
   It may MOST logically be concluded that

   A.  Programs K and L should be chosen to fit within the budget ceiling
   B.  Program K would be the most desirable one that could be afforded
   C.  Program M should be chosen rather than Program K
   D.  the choice should be between Programs M and K

3. If no assumptions can be made regarding the effects of change of scale, the MOST logi-       3.____
   cal conclusion, on the basis of the data available, is that

   A.  more data are needed for a budget choice of program
   B.  Program K is the most preferable because of its low cost and good benefit-to-cost
       ratio
   C.  Program M is the most preferable because of its high benefits and good benefit-to-
       cost ratio
   D.  there is no difference between Programs K and M, and either can be chosen for
       any purpose

# TEST 7

DIRECTIONS: Each question or incomplete statement is followed by several suggested answers or completions. Select the one that BEST answers the question or completes the statement. *PRINT THE LETTER OF THE CORRECT ANSWER IN THE SPACE AT THE RIGHT.*

Questions 1-6.

DIRECTIONS: Questions 1 through 6 are to be answered SOLELY on the basis of the information contained in the charts below which relate to the budget allocations of City X, a small suburban community. The charts depict the annual budget allocations by Department and by expenditures over a five-year period.

## CITY X BUDGET IN MILLIONS OF DOLLARS

### TABLE I. Budget Allocations By Department

| Department | 1997 | 1998 | 1999 | 2000 | 2001 |
|---|---|---|---|---|---|
| Public Safety | 30 | 45 | 50 | 40 | 50 |
| Health and Welfare | 50 | 75 | 90 | 60 | 70 |
| Engineering | 5 | 8 | 10 | 5 | 8 |
| Human Resources | 10 | 12 | 20 | 10 | 22 |
| Conservation & Environment | 10 | 15 | 20 | 20 | 15 |
| Education & Development | 15 | 25 | 35 | 15 | 15 |
| TOTAL BUDGET | 120 | 180 | 225 | 150 | 180 |

### TABLE II. Budget Allocations by Expenditures

| Category | 1997 | 1998 | 1999 | 2000 | 2001 |
|---|---|---|---|---|---|
| Raw Materials & Machinery | 36 | 63 | 68 | 30 | 98 |
| Capital Outlay | 12 | 27 | 56 | 15 | 18 |
| Personal Services | 72 | 90 | 101 | 105 | 64 |
| TOTAL BUDGET | 120 | 180 | 225 | 150 | 180 |

1. The year in which the SMALLEST percentage of the total annual budget was allocated to the Department of Education and Development is

   A. 1997      B. 1998      C. 2000      D. 2001

2. Assume that in 2000 the Department of Conservation and Environment divided its annual budget into the three categories of expenditures and in exactly the same proportion as the budget shown in Table II for the year 2000. The amount allocated for capital outlay in the Department of Conservation and Environment's 2000 budget was MOST NEARLY _____ million.

   A. $2      B. $4      C. $6      D. $10

3.  From the year 1998 to the year 2000, the sum of the annual budgets for the Departments        3._____
    of Public Safety and Engineering showed an overall _____ million.

    A.  decline; $8                          B.  increase; $7
    C.  decline; $15                         D.  increase; $22

4.  The LARGEST dollar increase in departmental budget allocations from one year to the           4._____
    next was in _____ from _____.

    A.  Public Safety; 1997 to 1998
    B.  Health and Welfare; 1997 to 1998
    C.  Education and Development; 1999 to 2000
    D.  Human Resources; 1999 to 2000

5.  During the five-year period, the annual budget of the Department of Human Resources            5._____
    was GREATER than the annual budget for the Department of Conservation and Environ-
    ment in _____ of the years.

    A.  none            B.  one              C.  two               D.  three

6.  If the total City X budget increases at the same rate from 2001 to 2002 as it did from         6._____
    2000 to 2001, the total City X budget for 2002 will be MOST NEARLY _____ million.

    A.  $180            B.  $200             C.  $210              D.  $215

# TEST 8

DIRECTIONS:   Each question or incomplete statement is followed by several suggested answers or completions. Select the one that BEST answers the question or completes the statement. *PRINT THE LETTER OF THE CORRECT ANSWER IN THE SPACE AT THE RIGHT.*

Questions 1-3.

DIRECTIONS:   Questions 1 through 3 are to be answered SOLELY on the basis of the following information.

Assume that in order to encourage Program A, the State and Federal governments have agreed to make the following reimbursements for money spent on Program A, provided the unreimbursed balance is paid from City funds.

During Fiscal Year 2001-2002 - For the first $2 million expended, 50% Federal reimbursement and 30% State reimbursement; for the next $3 million, 40% Federal reimbursement and 20% State reimbursement; for the next $5 million, 20% Federal reimbursement and 10% State reimbursement. Above $10 million expended, no Federal or State reimbursement.

During Fiscal Year 2002-2003 - For the first $1 million expended, 30% Federal reimbursement and 20% State reimbursement; for the next $4 million, 15% Federal reimbursement and 10% State reimbursement. Above $5 million expended, no Federal or State reimbursement.

1. Assume that the Program A expenditures are such that the State reimbursement for Fiscal Year 2001-2002 will be $1 million.
Then, the Federal reimbursement for Fiscal Year 2001-2002 will be

   A.  $1,600,000              B.  $1,800,000
   C.  $2,000,000              D.  $2,600,000

1._

2. Assume that $8 million were to be spent on Program A in Fiscal Year 2002-2003.
The TOTAL amount of unreimbursed City funds required would be

   A.  $3,500,000              B.  $4,500,000
   C.  $5,500,000              D.  $6,500,000

2._

3. Assume that the City desires to have a combined total of $6 million spent in Program A during both the Fiscal Year 2001-2002 and the Fiscal Year 2002-2003.
Of the following expenditure combinations, the one which results in the GREATEST reimbursement of City funds is _____ in Fiscal Year 2001-2002 and _____ in Fiscal Year 2002-2003.

   A.  $5 million; $1 million        B.  $4 million; $2 million
   C.  $3 million; $3 million        D.  $2 million; $4 million

3._

# KEY (CORRECT ANSWERS)

**TEST 1**

1. D
2. C
3. C

**TEST 2**

1. B
2. A
3. A
4. D

**TEST 3**

1. A
2. D
3. B

**TEST 4**

1. A
2. B
3. C
4. C

**TEST 5**

1. A
2. C
3. C

**TEST 6**

1. C
2. D
3. A

**TEST 7**

1. D
2. A
3. A
4. B
5. B
6. D

**TEST 8**

1. B
2. D
3. A

———

# PREPARING WRITTEN MATERIAL

## EXAMINATION SECTION
### TEST 1

DIRECTIONS : Each of the sentences in the tests that follow may be classified under one of the following four categories:

      A.  *Incorrect* because of faulty grammar or sentence structure
      B.  *Incorrect* because of faulty punctuation
      C.  *Incorrect* because of faulty capitalization
      D.  *Correct*

Examine each sentence carefully to determine under which of the above four options it is best classified. Then, in the space on the right, print the capital letter preceding the option which is the *BEST* of the four suggested above.
(Each incorrect sentence contains but one type of error. Consider a sentence to be correct if it contains none of the types of errors mentioned, even though there may be other correct ways of expressing the same thought.)

1. This fact, together with those brought out at the previous meeting, prove that the schedule is satisfactory to the employees.    1._____

2. Like many employees in scientific fields, the work of bookkeepers and accountants requires accuracy and neatness.    2._____

3. "What can I do for you," the secretary asked as she motioned to the visitor to take a seat.    3._____

4. Our representative, Mr. Charles will call on you next week to determine whether or not your claim has merit.    4._____

5. We expect you to return in the spring; please do not disappoint us.    5._____

6. Any supervisor, who disregards the just complaints of his subordinates, is remiss in the performance of his duty.    6._____

7. Because she took less than an hour for lunch is no reason for permitting her to leave before five o'clock.    7._____

8. "Miss Smith," said the supervisor, "Please arrange a meeting of the staff for two o'clock on Monday."    8._____

9. A private company's vacation and sick leave allowance usually differs considerably from a public agency.    9._____

10. Therefore, in order to increase the efficiency of operations in the department, a report on the recommended changes in procedures was presented to the departmental committee in charge of the program.    10._____

11. We told him to assign the work to whoever was available.    11._____

12. Since John was the most efficient of any other employee in the bureau, he received the highest service rating.    12._____

13. Only those members of the national organization who resided in the middle West     13.__
attended the conference in Chicago.

14. The question of whether the office manager has as yet attained, or indeed can ever hope     14.__
to secure professional status is one which has been discussed for years.

15. No one knew who to blame for the error which, we later discovered, resulted in a consid-     15.__
erable loss of time.

––––––––

# KEY (CORRECT ANSWERS)

| | | | |
|---|---|---|---|
| 1. | A | 6. | B |
| 2. | A | 7. | A |
| 3. | B | 8. | C |
| 4. | B | 9. | A |
| 5. | D | 10. | D |

| | |
|---|---|
| 11. | D |
| 12. | A |
| 13. | C |
| 14. | B |
| 15. | A |

––––––––

# TEST 2

1.  The National alliance of Businessmen is trying to persuade private businesses to hire youth in the summertime.                                                                                        1.____

2.  The supervisor who is on vacation, is in charge of processing vouchers.                      2.____

3.  The activity of the committee at its conferences is always stimulating.                      3.____

4.  After checking the addresses again, the letters went to the mailroom.                        4.____

5.  The director, as well as the employees, are interested in sharing the dividends.             5.____

———

# KEY (CORRECT ANSWERS)

1. C
2. B
3. D
4. A
5. A

———

# TEST 3

DIRECTIONS:   In each of the following groups of sentences, one of the four sentences is faulty in grammar, punctuation, or capitalization. Select the incorrect sentence in each case.

1.   A.   Sailing down the bay was a thrilling experience for me.          1._____
     B.   He was not consulted about your joining the club.
     C.   This story is different than the one I told you yesterday.
     D.   There is no doubt about his being the best player.

2.   A.   He maintains there is but one road to world peace.              2._____
     B.   It is common knowledge that a child sees much he is not supposed to see.
     C.   Much of the bitterness might have been avoided if arbitration had been resorted to earlier in the meeting.
     D.   The man decided it would be advisable to marry a girl somewhat younger than him.

3.   A.   In this book, the incident I liked least is where the hero tries to put out the forest fire.          3._____
     B.   Learning a foreign language will undoubtedly give a person a better understanding of his mother tongue.
     C.   His actions made us wonder what he planned to do next.
     D.   Because of the war, we were unable to travel during the summer vacation.

4.   A.   The class had no sooner become interested in the lesson than the dismissal bell rang.          4._____
     B.   There is little agreement about the kind of world to be planned at the peace conference.
     C.   "Today," said the teacher, "we shall read 'The Wind in the Willows.' I am sure you'll like it.
     D.   The terms of the legal settlement of the family quarrel handicapped both sides for many years.

5.   A.   I was so suprised that I was not able to say a word.          5._____
     B.   She is taller than any other member of the class.
     C.   It would be much more preferable if you were never seen in his company.
     D.   We had no choice but to excuse her for being late.

———

# KEY (CORRECT ANSWERS)

1. C
2. D
3. A
4. C
5. C

––––––

# TEST 4

DIRECTIONS:   In each of the following groups of sentences, one of the four sentences is faulty in grammar, punctuation, or capitalization. Select the incorrect sentence in each case.

1.   A.   Please send me these data at the earliest opportunity.          1.____
     B.   The loss of their material proved to be a severe handicap.
     C.   My principal objection to this plan is that it is impracticable .
     D.   The doll had laid in the rain for an hour and was ruined.

2.   A.   The garden scissors, left out all night in the rain, were in a badly rusted condition.   2.____
     B.   The girls felt bad about the misunderstanding which had arisen.
     C.   Sitting near the campfire, the old man told John and I about many exciting adventures he had had.
     D.   Neither of us is in a position to undertake a task of that magnitude.

3.   A.   The general concluded that one of the three roads would lead to the besieged city.   3.____
     B.   The children didn't, as a rule, do hardly anything beyond what they were told to do.
     C.   The reason the girl gave for her negligence was that she had acted on the spur of the moment.
     D.   The daffodils and tulips look beautiful in that blue vase.

4.   A.   If I was ten years older, I should be interested in this work.          4.____
     B.   Give the prize to whoever has drawn the best picture.
     C.   When you have finished reading the book, take it back to the library.
     D.   My drawing is as good as or better than yours.

5.   A.   He asked me whether the substance was animal or vegetable.          5.____
     B.   An apple which is unripe should not be eaten by a child.
     C.   That was an insult to me who am your friend.
     D.   Some spy must of reported the matter to the enemy.

6.   A.   Limited time makes quoting the entire message impossible.          6.____
     B.   Who did she say was going?
     C.   The girls in your class have dressed more dolls this year than we.
     D.   There was such a large amount of books on the floor that I couldn't find a place for my rocking chair.

7.   A.   What with his sleeplessness and his ill health, he was unable to assume any responsibility for the success of the meeting.   7.____
     B.   If I had been born in February, I should be celebrating my birthday soon.
     C.   In order to prevent breakage, she placed a sheet of paper between each of the plates when she packed them.
     D.   After the spring shower, the violets smelled very sweet.

8.   A.   He had laid the book down very reluctantly before the end of the lesson.   8.____
     B.   The dog, I am sorry to say, had lain on the bed all night.
     C.   The cloth was first lain on a flat surface; then it was pressed with a hot iron.
     D.   While we were in Florida, we lay in the sun until we were noticeably tanned.

9.  A.  If John was in New York during the recent holiday season, I have no doubt he spent most of his time with his parents.
    B.  How could he enjoy the television program; the dog was barking and the baby was crying.
    C.  When the problem was explained to the class, he must have been asleep.
    D.  She wished that her new dress were finished so that she could go to the party.

9.__

10. A.  The engine not only furnishes power but light and heat as well.
    B.  You're aware that we've forgotten whose guilt was established, aren't you?
    C.  Everybody knows that the woman made many sacrifices for her children.
    D.  A man with his dog and gun is a familiar sight in this neighborhood.

10.__

---

# KEY (CORRECT ANSWERS)

|    |   |     |   |
|----|---|-----|---|
| 1. | D | 6.  | D |
| 2. | C | 7.  | B |
| 3. | B | 8.  | C |
| 4. | A | 9.  | B |
| 5. | D | 10. | A |

---

# TEST 5

DIRECTIONS: Each of Questions 1 to 15 consists of a sentence which may be classified appropriately under one of the following four categories:
  A. *Incorrect* because of faulty grammar
  B. *Incorrect* because of faulty punctuation
  C. *Incorrect* because of faulty spelling
  D. *Correct*
Examine each sentence carefully. Then, print, in the space on the right, the letter preceding the category which is the best of the four suggested above.
  (Note: Each incorrect sentence contains only one type of error. Consider a sentence correct if it. contains no errors, although there may be other correct ways of writing the sentence.)

1. Of the two employees, the one in our office is the most efficient. 1._____

2. No one can apply or even understand, the new rules and regulations. 2._____

3. A large amount of supplies were stored in the empty office. 3._____

4. If an employee is occassionally asked to work overtime, he should do so willingly. 4._____

5. It is true that the new procedures are difficult to use but, we are certain that you will learn them quickly. 5._____

6. The office manager said that he did not know who would be given a large allotment under the new plan. 6._____

7. It was at the supervisor's request that the clerk agreed to postpone his vacation. 7._____

8. We do not believe that it is necessary for both he and the clerk to attend the conference. 8._____

9. All employees, who display perseverance, will be given adequate recognition. 9._____

10. He regrets that some of us employees are dissatisfied with our new assignments. 10._____

11. "Do you think that the raise was merited," asked the supervisor? 11._____

12. The new manual of procedure is a valuable supplament to our rules and regulations. 12._____

13. The typist admitted that she had attempted to pursuade the other employees to assist her in her work. 13._____

14. The supervisor asked that all amendments to the regulations be handled by you and I. 14._____

15. The custodian seen the boy who broke the window. 15._____

# KEY (CORRECT ANSWERS)

| | | | | |
|---|---|---|---|---|
| 1. | A | | 6. | D |
| 2. | B | | 7. | D |
| 3. | A | | 8. | A |
| 4. | C | | 9. | B |
| 5. | B | | 10. | D |

| | |
|---|---|
| 11. | B |
| 12. | C |
| 13. | C |
| 14. | A |
| 15. | A |

# EXAMINATION SECTION
## TEST 1

DIRECTIONS: Each question or incomplete statement is followed by several suggested answers or completions. Select the one that BEST answers the question or completes the statement. *PRINT THE LETTER OF THE CORRECT ANSWER IN THE SPACE AT THE RIGHT.*

Questions 1-4.

DIRECTIONS: Questions 1 through 4 are to be answered on the basis of the following passage.

A State department which is interested in finding acceptable solutions to the operational problems of specific types of community self-help organizations recently sent two of its staff members to meet with one such organization. At that meeting, the leaders of the community organization voiced the need for increased activity planning input of a more detailed nature from the citizens regularly served by that organization. There followed a discussion of a number of information-gathering methods, including surveys by telephone, questionnaires mailed to the citizens' residences, in-person interviews with the citizens, and the placing of suggestion boxes in the organization's headquarters building. Concern was expressed by one of the leaders that the organization's funds be spent judiciously. The State department representatives present promised to investigate the possibility of a matching fund grant of money to the organization.

Later, the proposed survey was conducted using questionnaires completed by those citizens who visited the organization's headquarters. The results of the survey included the information that twice as many citizens wanted more educational activities scheduled than wanted more social activities scheduled, whereas one-half of those who wanted more educational activities scheduled were interested mainly in special job training.

1. A similar survey conducted by a State department employee involved special job training. That survey uncovered the information below. The following four sentences are to be rearranged to form the most effective and logical paragraph. Select the letter representing the best sequence for these sentences.  
    I.   The majority of those who are still in this group are ethnic minorities.  
    II.  The number of economically disadvantaged people who enjoyed their special job training is larger than the number of economically disadvantaged people who did not enjoy it.  
    III.  Thirty-five percent of all those who are economically disadvantaged are not ethnic minorities.  
    IV.  Eighty percent of those who have completed special job training in the past ten years are economically disadvantaged.  
    The CORRECT answer is:

    A.  IV, I, III, II                B.  I, III, II, IV  
    C.  IV, II, I, III                D.  I, II, III, IV

1.\_\_\_\_

2. In the reading passage above, the word *judiciously* means MOST NEARLY

    A.  legally                     B.  immediately  
    C.  prudently                 D.  uniformly

2.\_\_\_\_

3. Based *only* on the information in the reading passage, which one of the following state-    3.__
   ments is MOST fully supported?

    A. The leaders of the community organization in question wanted to increase the
       quantity and quality of feedback about that organization's suggestion boxes.
    B. The number of citizens surveyed who wanted more educational activities sched-
       uled and were mainly interested in special job training was the same as the num-
       ber of citizens surveyed who wanted more social activities to be scheduled.
    C. At the meeting concerned, matching funds were promised to the community orga-
       nization in question by the two State department representatives present.
    D. Telephone surveys generally yield more accurate information than do surveys con-
       ducted through the use of mailed questionnaires.

4. The following four sentences are to be rearranged to form the most effective and logical    4.__
   paragraph. Select the letter representing the best sequence for these sentences.
    I.   Formal surveys of citizens within a community also convey to those citizens
         the interest of the community leadership in hearing the citizens' ideas about
         community improvement.
    II.  Such surveys can provide needed input into the process of establishing spe-
         cific community program goals.
    III. Formally conducted surveys of community residents often yield valuable
         information to the local area leaders responsible for community-based pro-
         grams.
    IV.  No community should formulate these goals without attempting to obtain the
         views of its citizenry.
   The CORRECT answer is:

    A. III, I, IV, II                      B. I, III, II, IV
    C. III, II, IV, I                      D. IV, III, II, I

Questions 5-8.

DIRECTIONS:   Questions 5 through 8 are to be answered on the basis of the following pas-
              sage.

The Smith Paint Company, which currently employs 2,000 persons, has been in existence for 20 years. A new chemical paint, Futuron, was recently developed by an employee of
that company. This paint was released for public use a month ago on a trial basis. The sales
were phenomenal, and there is a great demand for more Futuron to be manufactured. The
profits to be made by increased manufacturing and sale of Futuron could place the Smith
Paint Company in a leading role in the paint industry.

The Smith Paint Company currently produces 2 million gallons of the more traditional
paint per year. The Smith Paint Company's Board of Directors wishes to reduce its production
of this traditional paint by 50%, and to produce 1 million gallons of Futuron per year.

The employees are quite concerned about this potential production change. A public nonprofit research group has been investigating the chemical make-up of Futuron. Initial research indicates that negative physical reactions may result from working closely with the chemicals necessary to manufacture Futuron. For this reason, most of the company employees do not want the proposed change in production to occur. The members of the Board of Directors, however, argue that the research results are too inconclusive to cause great concern. They say that the company would lose 25% to 50% of its potential profit if the large-scale manufacturing of Futuron is not initiated immediately.

5. Seventy-five percent of the Smith Paint Company's current employees were hired during its first 10 years of operation. Fifteen percent were hired in the past five years. During the five-year interval between the first ten years and the most recent five years, 40 persons were hired per year.
   What percentage of its total employees were hired during the Smith Paint Company's first 13 years of operation?

   A. 75%          B. 81%          C. 85%          D. 90%

   5._____

6. Assume that the total possible profit the Smith Paint Company could make during its first year of manufacturing the proposed amount of Futuron would be $1.00 per gallon. The purchase of new machinery would reduce this first-year profit by 50%. The anticipated delay, during the first production year, in establishing large-scale manufacturing facilities would reduce the total possible profit by an additional 25%.
   Given this information, what would be the actual profit made from the first year of manufacturing Futuron?

   A. $250,000     B. $375,000     C. $500,000     D. $750,000

   6._____

7. In the reading passage, the word *inconclusive* means MOST NEARLY

   A. ineluctable              B. incorrect
   C. unreasonable            D. indeterminate

   7._____

8. Based on the information in the reading passage, which of the following statements represents the MOST accurate conclusion?

   A. The proposed reduction in the production of its traditional paint would not financially injure the Smith Paint Company.
   B. A greater proportion of the Smith Paint Company's employees are in favor of the proposed increase in Futuron production than are opposed to it.
   C. The increased Futuron production proposed by the Smith Paint Company's Board of Directors would cause that company's employees considerable health damage.
   D. Positive public response to the sale of Futuron suggests that considerable profit can be made by increasing the manufacturing and sale of Futuron.

   8._____

# KEY (CORRECT ANSWERS)

| | | | | |
|---|---|---|---|---|
| 1. | A | | 5. | B |
| 2. | C | | 6. | A |
| 3. | B | | 7. | D |
| 4. | C | | 8. | D |

―――――

# SOLUTIONS TO PROBLEMS

1.  For the following reasons, Choice A is correct and the other three choices are incorrect:

    1.  Both Choice B and Choice D begin with Sentence I, which states, *The majority of those who are still in this group are ethnic minorities.* The paragraph cannot logically begin with a statement such as Sentence I, because no one reading the paragraph would know what *this group* refers to. Therefore, Choice B and Choice D are not correct and may be eliminated from consideration.

    2.  Both Choice A and Choice C begin with Sentence IV, which states, *Eighty percent of those who have completed special job training in the past ten years are economically disadvantaged.* The problem then becomes selecting the best sequence of the other three sentences so that they most logically follow the initial Sentence IV.

    3.  If you select Choice C, then you are choosing Sentence II as the correct second sentence. Sentence II states, *The number of economically disadvantaged people who enjoyed their special job training is larger than the number of economically disadvantaged people who did not enjoy it.* Then Sentence I would be the third sentence. However, that would not be logical, because you could not tell whether *this group* in Sentence I refers to *economically disadvantaged people who enjoyed their special job training* or whether *this group* refers to *economically disadvantaged people who did not enjoy it.* Therefore, Choice C is not correct.

    4.  By the process of elimination, only Choice A remains. Choice A specifies Sentence I as the second sentence, which is logically correct in that *this group* in Sentence I will then refer to those who *are economically disadvantaged* in Sentence IV. The two remaining sentences also refer back to *economically disadvantaged,* thus creating a paragraph that reads logically from start to finish. Therefore, Choice A is the correct answer.

2.  Choices B and D should be eliminated from further consideration due to the context in which the word *judiciously* was used in the reading passage. Specifically, concern was expressed that funds be spent judiciously. Nothing in the paragraph suggests a need for concern if the funds were not spent immediately or uniformly. Choice A must be considered, because public funds should be spent legally. However, the word *judiciously* is related to the word *judgment* rather than to the word *judiciary.* It is the latter word that has to do with courts of law and is related to legality, so Choice A is incorrect. On the other hand, *judiciously* and *prudently* both mean *wisely* and *with direction.* Therefore, Choice C is correct.

3.  Choice B is the correct choice. No matter what numbers you apply, Choice B still will be correct. This is because when you multiply any number by two and then divide the result in half, you end up with the same number that you began with. For example, suppose that 20 citizens wanted more social activities. Twice that number (40 citizens) wanted more educational activities. But of those 40 citizens, one-half (20 citizens) wanted mainly special job training.

Choice A is incorrect because, first of all, the organization did not have any suggestion boxes; although suggestion boxes were discussed, questionnaires ultimately were used instead. In addition, Choice A is incorrect because it was input about the planning of activities that the leaders of the community organization wanted rather than feedback concerning suggestion boxes.

Choice C also is not correct. Instead of promising the matching funds, the State department representatives promised to investigate (or look into) the possibility of obtaining the matching funds.

Choice D is incorrect because the reading passage does not tell whether telephone surveys or mailed questionnaires provide more accurate information. Remember, the instructions for this question state that the question is to be answered based ONLY on the information in the applicable reading passage.

4. The correct answer is Choice C. Choice A and Choice C both begin with Sentence III, which certainly could be the logical first sentence of a paragraph. However, the next sentence (Sentence I) in Choice A leaves the initial topic of obtaining information from citizens. The third sentence in Choice A would be Sentence IV, *No community should formulate these goals without attempting to obtain the views of its citizenry.* The words *these goals* do not logically refer to anything in the previous two sentences, so Choice A is incorrect.

Choice B also is incorrect because the word *also* in its first sentence (Sentence I) has nothing to logically refer to. *Also* would have to be used in a sentence that comes later in the paragraph.

Choice D has the same problem as Choice A. Choice D begins with Sentence IV, which starts off, *No community should formulate these goals....* Again, the words *these goals* need to refer to something in a previous sentence about goals in order to be logically correct.

5. Choice B is correct. Here are the mathematical computations you might use to arrive at the correct answer of 81%:

1. The reading passage states that the Smith Paint Company currently employs 2,000 persons. The first part of this question states that 75% of those current employees were hired during the first ten years that the company was in operation. By multiplying 75% by 2,000, you would find that 1,500 of the current employees were hired during the company's first ten years.

2. The question asks about the first 13 years of the company's operation rather than just the first ten years. Therefore, you need the arithmetical information for the three years that immediately followed the first ten years. You know from the reading passage that the company has been operating for 20 years. You have the information for the first ten years. Twenty minus ten leaves the most recent ten years.

3.  You know from the question that 40 persons were hired each year during the five-year period of time between the first ten years and the most recent five years. However, you need information about only the first three years. By multiplying 40 persons per year by three years, you would find that 120 people were hired during the first three years that came immediately after the first ten years of the company's operation.

4.  Next, you would need to add 1,500 people (for the first ten years) and 120 people (for the next three years). That would give you a total of 1,620 people hired during the first 13 years.

5.  The question asks for the percentage of the Smith Paint Company's total employees hired during its first 13 years. You know that the total number of employees is 2,000. The question then is: 1,620 people is what percentage of 2,000 people? By dividing 2,000 into 1,620, you would find that the correct answer is 81%.

Choice A is incorrect because it deals with only the first ten years that the company was in operation, rather than the first 13 years. If you took 1,500 people (from Step 1 in the explanatory material for the correct answer) and divided that number by 2,000 people, you would arrive at 75%, which is not correct.

Choice C is incorrect. If you correctly arrived at 1,500 people for the first ten years but then incorrectly dealt with the next five years instead of the next three years, you would end up with the wrong answer of 85%. First, you would multiply 40 people by five years and end up with 200 people. Next, you would add 200 to 1,500 and end up with 1,700 people. Finally, you would divide 1,700 by 2,000 and get 85%.

Choice D also is incorrect. If you correctly arrived at 1,500 people for the first ten years but then used the information for the most recent five years instead of the information for the five years that came just before the most recent five years, you would end up with the incorrect answer of 90%. First, you would find from the question that 15% of the total employees were hired in the past five years. Next, you would multiply 15% by 2,000 total employees and end up with 300. Next, you would add 1,500 employees and 300 employees, ending up with a total of 1,800 employees. By dividing 1,800 by 2,000, you would arrive at 90%.

6.  Choice A is correct. Here are the mathematical computations you would need to make to arrive at the correct answer of $250,000:

    1.  The reading passage states that the amount of Futuron proposed for manufacture each year is 1 million gallons. The question states that the possible profit per gallon would be $1.00. By multiplying $1.00 by 1,000,000, you would find that $1,000,000 would be the total possible profit to be made during the first year.

    2.  The question states that the $1,000,000 possible profit would have to be reduced by 50% because of the purchase of new machinery, plus by an additional 25% due to the delay in establishing manufacturing facilities. The possible profit must, therefore, be reduced by 50% plus 25%, or by a total of 75%, leaving only 25% of the $1,000,000 as possible profit.

3. By multiplying 25% by $1,000,000, you would arrive at $250,000 as the actual profit which would be made.

Choice B is incorrect. If the two profit reductions were incorrectly multiplied by one another (50% times 25%) and the product (12 1/2%) added to 50%, there would have been a net reduction of 62 1/2%, yielding $375,000. However, the two profit reductions are independent of each other and should be added together.

Choice C also is incorrect. It would occur if you only took into account the 50% profit reduction. However, as the paragraph states, you must also deduct an additional 25% of the total profit.

Choice D ($750,000) would be made if you incorrectly multiplied the total profit reduction (75%) by $1,000,000. However, the question asks for the profit, not the profit reduction.

7. Both *indeterminate* and *inconclusive* mean *vague* and *indefinite,* so Choice D is correct. Choice A is incorrect, because the word *ineluctable* means inescapable or inevitable. The reading passage does not support the conclusion that the research results are incorrect or unreasonable, so Choice B and Choice C can be eliminated from consideration.

8. Choice D is correct. The reading passage states, *The sales were phenomenal, and there is a great demand for more Futuron to be manufactured. The profits to be made by increasing the manufacturing and sale of Futuron could place the Smith Paint Company in a leading role in the paint industry.* Since the sales of Futuron were phenomenal (remarkable; extraordinary), and there still is a great demand for it, the suggestion of considerable future profit is reasonable.

Choice A is not the most accurate conclusion based on the reading passage. The financial impact of decreasing the production of the traditional paint cannot be ascertained. Therefore, it is not certain that the proposed 50% reduction in the manufacturing of the Smith Paint Company's traditional paint would not financially injure that company. Certainly, Choice D is a more accurate conclusion.

Choice B is incorrect. A greater proportion of the employees being in favor of the proposed increase in Futuron production than not being in favor of it implies that over 50% of the employees are in favor of it. However, the reading passage states that most of the employees (which, logically, means over 50% of the employees) do not want the proposed change to occur.

Choice C also is not the most accurate conclusion. It states that the proposed increase in Futuron production would cause employees considerable health damage. The reading passage is not definite on this issue of health damage. It states, *Initial research indicates that negative physical reactions may result from working closely with the chemicals necessary....* How serious the health damage might be is not stated in the reading passage.

# PREPARING WRITTEN MATERIAL

# PARAGRAPH REARRANGEMENT
## COMMENTARY

The sentences which follow are in scrambled order. You are to rearrange them in proper order and indicate the letter choice containing the correct answer at the space at the right.

Each group of sentences in this section is actually a paragraph presented in scrambled order. Each sentence in the group has a place in that paragraph; no sentence is to be left out. You are to read each group of sentences and decide upon the best order in which to put the sentences so as to form as well-organized paragraph.

The questions in this section measure the ability to solve a problem when all the facts relevant to its solution are not given.

More specifically, certain positions of responsibility and authority require the employee to discover connections between events sometimes, apparently, unrelated. In order to do this, the employee will find it necessary to correctly infer that unspecified events have probably occurred or are likely to occur. This ability becomes especially important when action must be taken on incomplete information.

Accordingly, these questions require competitors to choose among several suggested alternatives, each of which presents a different sequential arrangement of the events. Competitors must choose the MOST logical of the suggested sequences.

In order to do so, they may be required to draw on general knowledge to infer missing concepts or events that are essential to sequencing the given events. Competitors should be careful to infer only what is essential to the sequence. The plausibility of the wrong alternatives will always require the inclusion of unlikely events or of additional chains of events which are NOT essential to sequencing the given events.

It's very important to remember that you are looking for the best of the four possible choices, and that the best choice of all may not even be one of the answers you're given to choose from.

There is no one right way to these problems. Many people have found it helpful to first write out the order of the sentences, as they would have arranged them, on their scrap paper before looking at the possible answers. If their optimum answer is there, this can save them some time. If it isn't, this method can still give insight into solving the problem. Others find it most helpful to just go through each of the possible choices, contrasting each as they go along. You should use whatever method feels comfortable, and works, for you.

While most of these types of questions are not that difficult, we've added a higher percentage of the difficult type, just to give you more practice. Usually there are only one or two questions on this section that contain such subtle distinctions that you're unable to answer confidently, and you then may find yourself stuck deciding between two possible choices, neither of which you're sure about.

———

# EXAMINATION SECTION
## TEST 1

DIRECTIONS: The sentences that follow are in scrambled order. You are to rearrange them in proper order and indicate the letter choice containing the correct answer. *PRINT THE LETTER OF THE CORRECT ANSWER IN THE SPACE AT THE RIGHT.*

1. Below are four statements labeled W., X., Y., and Z.    1._____
    W.    He was a strict and fanatic drillmaster.
    X.    The word is always used in a derogatory sense and generally shows resentment and anger on the part of the user.
    Y.    It is from the name of this Frenchman that we derive our English word, martinet.
    Z.    Jean Martinet was the Inspector-General of Infantry during the reign of King Louis XIV.
   The *PROPER* order in which these sentences should be placed in a paragraph is:

    A.  X, Z, W, Y        B.  X, Z, Y, W        C.  Z, W, Y, X        D.  Z, Y, W, X

2. In the following paragraph, the sentences which are numbered, have been jumbled.    2._____
    1.    Since then it has undergone changes.
    2.    It was incorporated in 1955 under the laws of the State of New York.
    3.    Its primary purpose, a cleaner city, has, however, remained the same.
    4.    The Citizens Committee works in cooperation with the Mayor's Inter-departmental Committee for a Clean City.
   The order in which these sentences should be arranged to form a well-organized paragraph is:

    A.  2, 4, 1, 3        B.  3, 4, 1, 2        C.  4, 2, 1, 3        D.  4, 3, 2, 1

Questions 3-5.

DIRECTIONS:    The sentences listed below are part of a meaningful paragraph but they are not given in their proper order. You are to decide what would be the *best order* in which to put the sentences so as to form a well-organized paragraph. Each sentence has a place in the paragraph; there are no extra sentences. You are then to answer questions 3 to 5 inclusive on the basis of your rearrangements of these secrambled sentences into a properly organized paragraph.

In 1887 some insurance companies organized an Inspection Department to advise their clients on all phases of fire prevention and protection. Probably this has been due to the smaller annual fire losses in Great Britain than in the United States. It tests various fire prevention devices and appliances and determines manufacturing hazards and their safeguards. Fire research began earlier in the United States and is more advanced than in Great Britain. Later they established a laboratory specializing in electrical, mechanical, hydraulic, and chemical fields.

3. When the five sentences are arranged in proper order, the paragraph starts with the sentence which begins

3.___

   A. "In 1887..."      B. "Probably this ..."      C. "It tests ..."
   D. "Fire research ..."     E. "Later they ..."

4. In the last sentence listed above, "they" refers to

4.___

   A. insurance companies
   B. the United States and Great Britain
   C. the Inspection Department
   D. clients
   E. technicians

5. When the above paragraph is properly arranged, it ends with the words

5.___

   A. "... and protection."      B. "... the United States."
   C. "... their safeguards."     D. "... in Great Britain."
   E. "... chemical fields."

___

# KEY (CORRECT ANSWERS)

   1. C
   2. C
   3. D
   4. A
   5. C

___

# TEST 2

DIRECTIONS: In each of the questions numbered 1 through 5, several sentences are given. For each question, choose as your answer the group of numbers that represents the *most logical* order of these sentences if they were arranged in paragraph form. *PRINT THE LETTER OF THE CORRECT ANSWER IN THE SPACE AT THE RIGHT.*

1.   1.   It is established when one shows that the landlord has prevented the tenant's enjoyment of his interest in the property leased.
    2.   Constructive eviction is the result of a breach of the covenant of quiet enjoyment implied in all leases.
    3.   In some parts of the United States, it is not complete until the tenant vacates within a reasonable time.
    4.   Generally, the acts must be of such serious and permanent character as to deny the tenant the enjoyment of his possessing rights.
    5.   In this event, upon abandonment of the premises, the tenant's liability for that ceases.

The CORRECT answer is:

A.   2, 1, 4, 3, 5      B.   5, 2, 3, 1, 4      C.   4, 3, 1, 2, 5
D.   1, 3, 5, 4, 2

1.____

2.   1.   The powerlessness before private and public authorities that is the typical experience of the slum tenant is reminiscent of the situation of blue-collar workers all through the nineteenth century.
    2.   Similarly, in recent years, this chapter of history has been reopened by anti-poverty groups which have attempted to organize slum tenants to enable them to bargain collectively with their landlords about the conditions of their tenancies.
    3.   It is familiar history that many of the workers remedied their condition by joining together and presenting their demands collectively.
    4.   Like the workers, tenants are forced by the conditions of modern life into substantial dependence on these who possess great political arid economic power.
    5.   What's more, the very fact of dependence coupled with an absence of education and self-confidence makes them hesitant and unable to stand up for what they need from those in power.

The CORRECT answer is:

A.   5, 4, 1, 2, 3      B.   2, 3, 1, 5, 4      C.   3, 1, 5, 4, 2
D.   1, 4, 5, 3, 2

2.____

3.   1.   A railroad, for example, when not acting as a common carrier may contract; away responsibility for its own negligence.
    2.   As to a landlord, however, no decision has been found relating to the legal effect of a clause shifting the statutory duty of repair to the tenant.
    3.   The courts have not passed on the validity of clauses relieving the landlord of this duty and liability.
    4.   They have, however, upheld the validity of exculpatory clauses in other types of contracts.
    5.   Housing regulations impose a duty upon the landlord to maintain leased premises in safe condition.

3.____

6. As another example, a bailee may limit his liability except for gross negligence, willful acts, or fraud.

The CORRECT answer is:

A. 2, 1, 6, 4, 3, 5      B. 1, 3, 4, 5, 6, 2      C. 3, 5, 1, 4, 2, 6
D. 5, 3, 4, 1, 6, 2

4.  1. Since there are only samples in the building, retail or consumer sales are generally eschewed by mart occupants, and,in some instances, rigid controls are maintained to limit entrance to the mart only to those persons engaged in retailing.
    2. Since World War I, in many larger cities, there has developed a new type of property, called the mart building.
    3. It can, therefore, be used by wholesalers and jobbers for the display of sample merchandise.
    4. This type of building is most frequently a multi-storied, finished interior property which is a cross between a retail arcade and a loft building.
    5. This limitation enables the mart occupants to ship the orders from another location after the retailer or dealer makes his selection from the samples.

4.___

The CORRECT answer is:

A. 2, 4, 3, 1, 5      B. 4, 3, 5, 1, 2      C. 1, 3, 2, 4, 5
D. 1, 4, 2, 3, 5

5.  1. In general, staff-line friction reduces the distinctive contribution of staff personnel.
    2. The conflicts, however, introduce an uncontrolled element into the managerial system.
    3. On the other hand, the natural resistance of the line to staff innovations probably usefully restrains over-eager efforts to apply untested procedures on a large scale.
    4. Under such conditions, it is difficult to know when valuable ideas are being sacrificed.
    5. The relatively weak position of staff, requiring accommodation to the line, tends to restrict their ability to engage .in free, experimental innovation.

5.___

The CORRECT answer is:

A. 4, 2, 3, 1, 3      B. 1, 5, 3, 2, 4      C. 5, 3, 1, 2, 4
D. 2, 1, 4, 5, 3

———

# KEY (CORRECT ANSWERS)

1. A
2. D
3. D
4. A
5. B

———

# TEST 3

DIRECTIONS: Questions 1 through 4 consist of six sentences which can be arranged in a logical sequence. For each question, select the choice which places the numbered sentences in the *most logical* sequence. *PRINT THE LETTER OF THE CORRECT ANSWER IN THE SPACE AT THE RIGHT.*

1.    1. The burden of proof as to each issue is determined before trial and remains upon the same party throughout the trial.
     2. The jury is at liberty to believe one witness' testimony as against a number of contradictory witnesses.
     3. In a civil case, the party bearing the burden of proof is required to prove his contention by a fair preponderance of the evidence.
     4. However, it must be noted that a fair preponderance of evidence does not necessarily mean a greater number of witnesses.
     5. The burden of proof is the burden which rests upon one of the parties to an action to persuade the trier of the facts, generally the jury, that a proposition he asserts is true.
     6. If the evidence is equally balanced, or if it leaves the jury in such doubt as to be unable to decide the controversy either way, judgment must be given against the party upon whom the burden of proof rests.

1.\_\_\_\_

     The CORRECT answer is:

     A.   3, 2, 5, 4, 1, 6      B.   1, 2, 6, 5, 3, 4      C.   3, 4, 5, 1, 2, 6
     D.   5, 1, 3, 6, 4, 2

2.    1. If a parent is without assets and is unemployed, he cannot be convicted of the crime of non-support of a child.
     2. The term "sufficient ability" has been held to mean sufficient financial ability.
     3. It does not matter if his unemployment is by choice or unavoidable circumstances.
     4. If he fails to take any steps at all, he may be liable to prosecution for endangering the welfare of a child.
     5. Under the penal law, a parent is responsible for the support of his minor child only if the parent is "of sufficient ability."
     6. An indigent parent may meet his obligation by borrowing money or by seeking aid under the provisions of the Social Welfare Law.

2.\_\_\_\_

     The CORRECT answer is:

     A.   6, 1, 5, 3, 2, 4      B.   1, 3, 5, 2, 4, 6      C.   5, 2, 1, 3, 6, 4
     D.   1, 6, 4, 5, 2, 3

3.  1. Consider, for example, the case of a rabble rouser who urges a group of twenty people to go out and break the windows of a nearby factory.
    2. Therefore, the law fills the indicated gap with the crime of inciting to riot."
    3. A person is considered guilty of inciting to riot when he urges ten or more persons to engage in tumultuous and violent conduct of a kind likely to create public alarm.
    4. However, if he has not obtained the cooperation of at least four people, he cannot be charged with unlawful assembly.
    5. The charge of inciting to riot was added to the law to cover types of conduct which cannot be classified as either the crime of "riot" or the crime of "unlawful assembly."
    6. If he acquires the acquiescence of at least four of them, he is guilty of unlawful assembly even if the project does not materialize.

The CORRECT answer is:

A. 3, 5, 1, 6, 4, 2      B. 5, 1, 4, 6, 2, 3      C. 3, 4, 1, 5, 2, 6
D. 5, 1, 4, 6, 3, 2

3.___

4.  1. If, however, the rebuttal evidence presents an issue of credibility, it is for the jury to determine whether the presumption has, in fact, been destroyed.
    2. Once sufficient evidence to the contrary is introduced, the presumption disappears from the trial.
    3. The effect of a presumption is to place the burden upon the adversary to come forward with evidence to rebut the presumption.
    4. When a presumption is overcome and ceases to exist in the case, the fact or facts which gave rise to the presumption still remain.
    5. Whether a presumption has been overcome is ordinarily a question for the court.
    6. Such information may furnish a basis for a logical inference.

The CORRECT answer is:

A. 4, 6, 2, 5, 1, 3      B. 3, 2, 5, 1, 4, 6      C. 5, 3, 6, 4, 2, 1
D. 5, 4, 1, 2, 6, 3

4.___

---

# KEY (CORRECT ANSWERS)

1. D
2. C
3. A
4. B

---

# BASIC FUNDAMENTALS OF A FINANCIAL STATEMENT

## TABLE OF CONTENTS

# BASIC FUNDAMENTALS
# OF A FINANCIAL STATEMENT

## COMMENTARY

The ability to read and understand a financial statement is a basic requirement for the accountant, auditor, account clerk, bookkeeper, bank examiner. budget examiner, and, of course, for the executive who must manage and administer departmental affairs.

## FINANCIAL REPORTS

Are financial reports really as difficult as all that? Well, if you know they are not so difficult because you have worked with them before, this section will be of auxiliary help for you. However, if you find financial statements a bit murky, but realize their great importance to you, we ought to get along fine together. For "mathematics," all we'll use is fourth-grade arithmetic.

Accountants, like all other professionals, have developed a specialized vocabulary. Sometimes this is helpful and sometimes plain confusing (like their practice of calling the income account, "Statement of Profit and Loss," when it is bound to be one or the other). But there are really only a score or so technical terms that you will have to get straight in mind. After that is done, the whole foggy business will begin to clear and in no time at all you'll be able to talk as wisely as the next fellow.

## BALANCE SHEET

Look at the sample balance sheet printed on page 2, and we'll have an insight into how it is put together. This particular report is neither the simplest that could be issued, nor the most complicated. It is a good average sample of the kind of report issued by an up-to-date manufacturing company.

Note particularly that the *balance sheet* represents the situation as it stood on one particular day, December 31, not the record of a year's operation. This balance sheet is broken into two parts: on the left are shown *ASSETS* and on the right *LIABILITIES*. Under the asset column, you will find listed the value of things the company owns or are owed to the company. Under liabilities, are listed the things the company owes to others, plus reserves, surplus, and the stated value of the stockholders' interest in the company.

One frequently hears the comment, "Well, I don't see what a good balance sheet is anyway, because the assets and liabilities are always the same whether the company is successful or not."

It is true that they always balance and, by itself, a balance sheet doesn't tell much until it is analyzed. Fortunately, we can make a balance sheet tell its story without too much effort -- often an extremely revealing story, particularly, if we compare the records of several years. ASSETS The first notation on the asset side of the balance sheet is *CURRENT* ASSETS (item 1). In general, current assets include cash and things that can be turned into cash in a hurry, or that, in the normal course of business, will be turned into cash in the reasonably near future, usually within a year.

Item 2 on our sample sheet is *CASH.* Cash is just what you would expect -bills and silver in the till and money on deposit in the bank.

*UNITED STATES GOVERNMENT SECURITIES* is item 3. The general practice is to show securities listed as current assets at cost or market value, whichever is lower. The figure, for all reasonable purposes, represents the amount by which total cash could be easily increased if the company wanted to sell these securities.

The next entry is *ACCOUNTS RECEIVABLE* (item 4). Here we find the total amount of money owed to the company by its regular business creditors and collectable within the next year. Most of the money is owed to the company by its customers for goods that the company

1

delivered on credit. If this were a department store instead of a manufacturer, what you owed the store on your charge account would be included here. Because some people fail to pay their bills, the company sets up a reserve for doubtful accounts, which it subtracts from all the money owed.

## THE ABC MANUFACTURING COMPANY, INC.
## CONSOLIDATED BALANCE SHEET – DECEMBER 31

| Item | | | | Item | | | | |
|------|---|---|---|------|---|---|---|---|
| 1. CURRENT ASSETS | | | | 16. CURRENT LIABILITIES | | | | |
| 2. Cash | | | | 17. Accts. Payable | | $ 300,000 | | |
| 3. U.S. Government Securities | | | | 18. Accrued Taxes | | 800,000 | | |
| 4. Accounts Receivable (less reserves) | 2,000,000 | | | 19. Accrued Wages, Interest and Other Expenses | | 370,000 | | |
| 5. Inventories (at lower of cost or market) | 2,000,000 | | | 20. Total Current Liabilities | | $1,470,000 | | |
| 6. Total Current Assets | $7,000,000 | | | 21. FIRST MORTGAGE SINK-ING FUND BONDS, 3 1/2% DUE 2002 | | 2,000,000 | | |
| 7. INVESTMENT IN AFFIL-IATED COMPANY Not consolidated (at cost, not in excess of net assets) | 200,000 | | | 22. RESERVE FOR CON-TINGENCIES | | 200,000 | | |
| 8. OTHER INVESTMENTS At cost, less than market | 100,000 | | | 23. CAPITAL STOCK: | | | | |
| 9. PLANT IMPROVEMENT FUND | 550,000 | | | 24. 5% Preferred Stock (author-ized and issued 10,000 shares of $100 par value) | $1,000,000 | | | |
| 10. PROPERTY, PLANT AND EQUIPMENT: Cost | $8,000,000 | | | 25. Common stock (author-ized and issued 400,000 shares of no par value) | 1,000,000 | 2,000,000 | | |
| 11. Less Reserve for Deprecia-tion | 5,000,000 | | | 26. SURPLUS: | | | | |
| 12. NET PROPERTY | 3,000,000 | | | 27. Earned | 3,530,000 | | | |
| 13. PREPAYMENTS | 50,000 | | | 28. Capital (arising from sale of common capital stock at price in excess of stated value | 1,900,000 | | | |
| 14. DEFERRED CHARGES | 100,000 | | | | | 5,430,000 | | |
| 15. PATENTS AND GOODWILL | 100,000 | | | | | | | |
| TOTAL | $11,100,000 | | | TOTAL | | $11,100,000 | | |

Item 5, *INVENTORIES,* is the value the company places on the supplies it owns. The inventory of a manufacturer may contain raw materials that it uses in making the things it sells, partially finished goods in process of manufacture and, finally, completed merchandise that it is ready to sell. Several methods are used to arrive at the value placed on these various items. The most common is to value them at their cost or present market value, whichever is lower. You can be reasonably confident, however, that the figure given is an honest and significant one for the particular industry if the report is certified by a reputable firm of public accountants.

Next on the asset side is *TOTAL CURRENT ASSETS* (item 6). This is an extremely important figure when used in connection with other items in the report, which we will come to presently. Then we will discover how to make total current assets tell their story.

*INVESTMENT IN AFFILIATED COMPANY* (item 7) represents the cost to our parent company of the capital stock of its *subsidiary* or affiliated company. A subsidiary is simply one company that is controlled by another. Most corporations that own other companies outright, lump the figures in a *CONSOLIDATED BALANCE SHEET.* This means that, under cash, for example, one would find a total figure that represented *all* of the cash of the parent company and of its wholly owned subsidiary. This is a perfectly reasonable procedure because, in the last analysis, all of the money is controlled by the same persons.

Our typical company shows that it has *OTHER INVESTMENTS* (item 8), in addition to its affiliated company. Sometimes good marketable securities other than Government bonds are carried as current assets, but the more conservative practice is to list these other security holdings separately. If they have been bought as a permanent investment, they would always be shown by themselves. "At cost, less than market" means that our company paid $100,000 for these other investments, but they are now worth more.

Among our assets is a *PLANT IMPROVEMENT FUND* (item 9). Of course, this item does not appear in all company balance sheets, but is typical of *special funds* that companies set up for one purpose or another. For example, money set aside to pay off part of the bonded debt of a company might be segregated into a special fund. The money our directors have put aside to improve the plant would often be invested in Government bonds.

## FIXED ASSETS

The next item (10), is *PROPERTY, PLANT AND EQUIPMENT,* but it might just as well be labeled *Fixed Assets* as these terms are used more or less interchangeably. Under item 10, the report gives the value of land, buildings, and machinery and such movable things as trucks, furniture, and hand tools. Historically, probably more sins were committed against this balance sheet item than any other.

In olden days, cattlemen used to drive their stock to market in the city. It was a common trick to stop outside of town, spread out some salt for the cattle to make them thirsty and then let them drink all the water they could hold. When they were weighed for sale, the cattlemen would collect cash for the water the stock had drunk. Business buccaneers, taking the cue from their farmer friends, would often "write up" the value of their fixed assets. In other words, they would increase the value shown on the balance sheet, making the capital stock appear to be worth a lot more than it was. *Watered stock* proved a bad investment for most stockholders. The practice has, fortunately, been stopped, though it took major financial reorganizations to squeeze the water out of some securities.

The most common practice today is to list fixed assets at cost. Often, there is no ready market for most of the things that fall under this heading, so it is not possible to give market value. A good report will tell what is included under fixed assets and how it has been valued. If the value has been increased by *write-up* or decreased by *write-down,* a footnote explanation is usually given. A *write-up* might occur, for instance, if the value of real estate increased substantially. A *write-down* might follow the invention of a new machine that put an important part of the company's equipment out of date.

## DEPRECIATION

Naturally, all of the fixed property of a company will wear out in time (except, of course, non-agricultural land). In recognition of this fact, companies set up a *RESERVE FOR DEPRECIATION* (item 11). If a truck costs $4,000 and is expected to last four years, it will be depreciated at the rate of $1,000 a year.

Two other terms also frequently occur in connection with depreciation -*depletion* and *obsolescence*. Companies may lump depreciation, depletion, and obsolescence under a single title, or list them separately.

*Depletion* is a term used primarily by mining and oil companies (or any of the so-called extractive industries). Depletion means exhaust or use up. As the oil or other natural resource is used up, a reserve is set up, to compensate for the natural wealth the company no longer owns. This reserve is set up in recognition of the fact that, as the company sells its natural product, it must get back not only the cost of extracting but also the original cost of the natural resource.

*Obsolescence* represents the loss in value because a piece of property has gone out of date before it wore out. Airplanes are modern examples of assets that tend to get behind the times long before the parts wear out. (Women and husbands will be familiar with the speed at which ladies' hats "obsolesce.")

In our sample balance sheet we have placed the reserve for depreciation under fixed assets and then subtracted, giving us *NET PROPERTY* (item 12), which we add into the asset column. Sometimes, companies put the reserve for depreciation in the liability column. As you can see, the effect is just the same whether it is *subtracted* from assets or *added* to liabilities.

The manufacturer, whose balance sheet we use, rents a New York showroom and pays his rent yearly, in advance. Consequently, he has listed under assets *PREPAYMENTS* (item 13). This is listed as an asset because he has paid for the use of the showroom, but has not yet received the benefit from its use. The use is something coming to the firm in the following year and, hence, is an asset. The dollar value of this asset will decrease by one-twelfth each month during the coming year.

*DEFERRED CHARGES* (item 14) represents a type of expenditure similar to prepayment. For example, our manufacturer brought out a new product last year, spending $100,000 introducing it to the market. As the benefit from this expenditure will be returned over months or even years to come, the manufacturer did not think it reasonable to charge the full expenditure against costs during the year. He has *deferred* the charges and will write them off gradually.

## INTANGIBLES

The last entry in our asset column is *PATENTS AND GOODWILL* (item 15). If our company were a young one, set up to manufacture some new patented prod uct, it would probably carry its patents at a substantial figure. In fact, *intangibles* of both old and new companies are often of great but generally unmeasurable worth.

Company practice varies considerably in assigning value to intangibles. Procter & Gamble, despite the tremendous goodwill that has been built up for IVORY SOAP, has reduced all of its intangibles to the nominal $1. Some of the big cigarette companies, on the contrary, place a high dollar value on the goodwill their brand names enjoy. Companies that spend a good deal for research and the development of new products are more inclined than others to reflect this fact in the value assigned to patents, license agreements, etc.

## LIABILITIES

The liability side of the balance sheet appears a little deceptive at first glance. Several of the entries simply don't sound like liabilities by any ordinary definition of the term.

The first term on the liability side of any balance sheet is usually CURRENT LIABILITIES (item 16). This is a companion to the *Current Assets* item across the page and includes all debts that fall due within the next year. The relation between current assets and current liabilities is one of the most revealing things to be gotten from the balance sheet, but we will go into that quite thoroughly later on.

*ACCOUNTS PAYABLE* (item 17) represents the money that the company owes to its ordinary business creditors -- unpaid bills for materials, supplies, insurance, and the like. Many companies itemize the money they owe in a much more detailed fashion than we have done, but, as you will see, the totals are the most interesting thing to us.

Item 18, *ACCRUED TAXES,* is the tax bill that the company estimates it still owes for the past year. We have lumped all taxes in our balance sheet, as many companies do. However, sometimes you will find each type of tax given separately. If the detailed procedure is followed, the description of the tax is usually quite sufficient to identify the separate items.

Accounts Payable was defined as the money the company owed to its regular business creditors. The company also owes, on any given day, wages to its own employees; interest to its bondholders and to banks from which it may have borrowed money; fees to its attorneys; pensions, etc. These are all totaled under *ACCRUED WAGES, INTEREST AND OTHER EXPENSES* (item 19).

*TOTAL CURRENT LIABILITIES* (item 20) is just the sum of everything that the company owed on December 31 and which must be paid sometime in the next twelve months.

It is quite clear that all of the things discussed above are liabilities. The rest of the entries on the liability side of the balance sheet, however, do not seem at first glance to be liabilities.

Our balance sheet shows that the company, on December 31, had $2,000,000 of 3 1/2 percent First Mortgage *BONDS* outstanding (item 21). Legally, the money received by a company when it sells bonds is considered a loan to the company. Therefore, it is obvious that the company owes to the bondholders an amount equal to the face value or the *call price* of the bonds it has outstanding. The call price is a figure usually larger than the face value of the bonds at which price the company can *call* the bonds in from the bondholders and pay them off before they ordinarily fall due. The date that often occurs as part of the name of a bond is the date at which the company has promised to pay off the loan from the bondholders.

## RESERVES

The next heading, *RESERVE FOR CONTINGENCIES* (item 22), sounds more like an asset than a liability. "My reserves," you might say, "are dollars in the bank, and dollars in the bank are assets."

No one would deny that you have something there. In fact, the corporation treasurer also has his reserve for contingencies balanced by either cash or some kind of unspecified investment on the asset side of the ledger. His reason for setting up a reserve on the liability side of the balance sheet is a precaution against making his financial position seem better than it is. He decided that the company might have to pay out this money during the coming year if certain things happened. If he did not set up the "reserve," his surplus would appear larger by an amount equal to his reserve.

A very large reserve for contingencies or a sharp increase in this figure from the previous year should be examined closely by the investor. Often, in the past, companies tried to hide their true earnings by transferring funds into a contingency reserve. As a reserve looks somewhat like a true liability, stockholders were confused about the real value of their securities. When a reserve is not set up for protection against some very probable loss or expenditure, it should be considered by the investor as part of surplus.

## CAPITAL STOCK

Below reserves there is a major heading, *CAPITAL STOCK* (item 23). Companies may have one type of security outstanding, or they may have a dozen. All of the issues that represent shares of ownership are capital, regardless of what they are called on the balance sheet -- preferred stock, preference stock, common stock, founders' shares, capital stock, or something else.

Our typical company has one issue of 5 per cent *PREFERRED STOCK* (item 24). It is called *preferred* because those who own it have a right to dividends and assets before the *common* stockholders -- that is, the holders are in a preferred position as owners. Usually, preferred stockholders do not have a voice in company affairs unless the company fails to pay them dividends at the promised rate. Their rights to dividends are almost always *cumulative.* This simply means that all past dividends must be paid before the other stockholders can receive anything. Preferred stockholders are not creditors of the company so it cannot properly be said that the company *owes* them the value of their holdings. However, in case the company decided to go out of business, preferred stockholders would have a prior claim on anything that was left in the company treasury after all of the creditors, including the bondholders, were paid off. In practice, this right does not always mean much, but it does explain why the book value of their holdings is carried as a liability.

*COMMON STOCK* (item 25) is simple enough as far as definition is concerned it represents the rights of the ordinary owner of the company. Each company has as many owners as it has stockholders. The proportion of the company that each stockholder owns is determined by the number of shares he has. However, neither the book value of a no-par common stock, nor the par value of an issue that has a given par, can be considered as representing either the original sale price, the market value, or what would be left for the stockholders if the company were liquidated.

A profitable company will seldom be dissolved. Once things have taken such a turn that dissolution appears desirable, the stated value of the stock is generally nothing but a fiction. Even if the company is profitable as a going institution, once it ceases to function even its tangible assets drop in value because there is not usually a ready market for its inventory of raw materials and semi-finished goods, or its plant and machinery.

## SURPLUS

The last major heading on the liability side of the balance sheet is *SURPLUS* (item 26). The surplus, of course, is not a liability in the popular sense at all. It represents, on our balance sheet, the difference between the stated value of our common stock and the net assets behind the stock.

Two different kinds of surplus frequently appear on company balance sheets, and our company has both kinds. The first type listed is *EARNED* surplus (item 27). Earned surplus is roughly similar to your own savings. To the corporation, earned surplus is that part of net income which has not been paid to stockholders as dividends. It still *belongs* to you, but the directors have decided that it is best for the company and the stockholders to keep it in the business. The surplus may be invested in the plant just as you might invest part of your savings in your home. It may also be in cash or securities.

In addition to the earned surplus, our company also has a *CAPITAL* surplus (item 28) of $1,900.00, which the balance sheet explains arose from selling the stock at a higher cost per share than is given as its stated value. A little arithmetic shows that the stock is carried on the books at $2.50 a share while the capital surplus amounts to $4.75 a share. From this we know that the company actually received an average of $7.25 net a share for the stock when it was sold.

# WHAT DOES THE BALANCE SHEET SHOW?

Before we undertake to analyze the balance sheet figures, a word on just what an investor can expect to learn is in order. A generation or more ago, before present accounting standards had gained wide acceptance, considerable imagination went into the preparation of balance sheets. This, naturally, made the public skeptical of financial reports. Today, there is no substantial ground for skepticism. The certified public accountant, the listing requirements of the national stock exchanges, and the regulations of the Securities and Exchange Commission have, for all practical purposes, removed the grounds for doubting the good faith of financial reports.

The investor, however, is still faced with the task of determining the significance of the figures. As we have already seen, a number of items are based, to a large degree, upon estimates, while others are, of necessity, somewhat arbitrary.

# NET WORKING CAPITAL

There is one very important thing that we can find from the balance sheet and accept with the full confidence that we know what we are dealing with. That is net working capital, sometimes simply called working capital.

On the asset side of our balance sheet we have added up all of the current assets and show the total as item 6. On the liability side, item 20 gives the total of current liabilities. *Net working capital* or *net current assets* is the difference left after subtracting current liabilities from current assets. If you consider yourself an investor rather than a speculator, you should always insist that any company in which you invest have a comfortable amount of working capital. The ability of a company to meet its obligations with ease, expand its volume as business expands and take advantage of opportunities as they present themselves, is, to an important degree, determined by its working capital.

Probably the question in your mind is: *"Just what does 'comfortable amount' of working capital mean?"* Well, there are several methods used by analysts to judge whether a particular company has a sound working capital position. The first rough test for an industrial company is to compare the working capital figure with the current liability total. Most analysts say that minimum safety requires that net working capital at least equal current liabilities. Or, put another way, that current assets should be at least twice as large as current liabilities.

There are so many different kinds of companies, however, that this test requires a great deal of modification if it is to be really helpful in analyzing companies in different industries. To help you interpret the *current position* of a company in which you are considering investing, the *current ratio* is more helpful than the dollar total of working capital. The current ratio is current assets divided by current liabilities.

In addition to working capital and current ratio, there are two other ways of testing the adequacy of the current position. *Net quick assets* provide a rigorous and important test of a company's ability to meet its current obligations. Net quick assets are found by taking total current assets (item 6) and subtracting the value of inventories (item 5). A well-fixed industrial company should show a reasonable excess of quick assets over current liabilities..

Finally, many analysts say that a good industrial company should have at least as much working capital (current assets less current liabilities) as the total book value of its bonds and preferred stock. In other words, current liabilities, bonded debt, and preferred stock *altogether* should not exceed the current assets.

## INVENTORY AND INVENTORY TURNOVER

In the recent past, there has been much talk of inventories. Many commentators have said that these carry a serious danger to company earnings if management allows them to increase too much. Of course, this has always been true, but present high prices have made everyone more inventory-conscious than usual.

There are several dangers in a large inventory position. In the first place, a sharp drop in price may cause serious losses; also, a large inventory may indicate that the company has accumulated a big supply of unsalable merchandise. The question still remains, however: *"What do we mean by large inventory?"*

As you certainly realize, an inventory is large or small only in terms of the yearly turnover and the type of business. We can discover the annual turnover of our sample company by dividing inventories (item 5) into total annual sales (item "a" on the income account).

It is also interesting to compare the value of the inventory of a company being studied with total current assets. Again, however, there is considerable variation between different types of companies, so that the relationship becomes significant only when compared with similar companies.

## NET BOOK VALUE OF SECURITIES

There is one other very important thing that can be gotten from the balance sheet, and that is the net book or equity value of the company's securities. We can calculate the net book value of each of the three types of securities our company has outstanding by a little very simple arithmetic. *Book value means the value at which something is carried on the books of the company.*

The full rights of the bondholders come before any of the rights of the stockholders, so, to find the net book value or net tangible assets backing up the bonds we add together the balance sheet value of the bonds, preferred stock, common stock, reserve, and surplus. This gives us a total of $9,630,000. (We would not include contingency reserve if we were reasonably sure the contingency was going to arise, but, as general reserves are often equivalent to surplus, it is, usually, best to treat the reserve just as though it were surplus.) However, part of this value represents the goodwill and patents carried at $100,000, which is not a tangible item, so, to be conservative, we subtract this amount, leaving $9,530,000 as the total net book value of the bonds. This is equivalent to $4,765 for each $1,000 bond, a generous figure. To calculate the net book value of the preferred stock, we must eliminate the face value of the bonds, and then, following the same procedure, add the value of the preferred stock, common stock, reserve, and surplus, and subtract goodwill. This gives us a total net book value for the preferred stock of $7,530,000 or $753 for each share of $100 par value preferred. This is also very good coverage for the preferred stock, but we must examine current earnings before becoming too enthusiastic about the *value* of any security.

The net book value of the common stock, while an interesting figure, is not so important as the coverage on the senior securities. In case of liquidation, there is seldom much left for the common stockholders because of the normal loss in value of company assets when they are put up for sale, as mentioned before. The book value figure, however, does give us a basis for comparison with other companies. Comparisons of net book value over a period of years also show us if the company is a soundly growing one or, on the other hand, is losing ground. Earnings, however, are our important measure of common stock values, as we will see shortly.

The net book value of the common stock is found by adding the stated value of the common stock, reserves, and surplus and then subtracting patents and goodwill. This gives us a total net book value of $6,530,000. As there are 400,000 shares of common outstanding, each share has a net book value of $16.32. You must be careful not to be misled by book value figures, particularly of common stock. Profitable companies (Coca-Cola, for example) often show a very low net book value and very substantial earnings. Railroads, on the other hand, may show a high book value for their common stock but have such low or irregular earnings that the market price of the stock is much less than its apparent book value. Banks, insurance companies, and investment -trusts are exceptions to what we have said about common stock net book value. As their assets are largely liquid (i.e., cash, accounts receivable, and marketable securities), the book value of their common stock sometimes indicates its value very accurately.

## PROPORTION OF BONDS, PREFERRED AND COMMON STOCK

Before investing, you will want to know the proportion of each kind of security issued by the company you are considering. A high proportion of bonds reduces the attractiveness of both the preferred and common stock, while too large an amount of preferred detracts from the value of the common.

The *bond ratio* is found by dividing the face value of the bonds (item 21), or $2,000,000, by the total value of the bonds, preferred stock, common stock, reserve, and surplus, or $9,630,000. This shows that bonds amount to about 20 per cent of the total of bonds, capital, and surplus.

The *preferred stock ratio* is found in the same way, only we divide the stated value of the preferred stock by the total of the other five items. Since we have half as much preferred stock as we have bonds, the preferred ratio is roughly 10.

Naturally, the *common stock ratio* will be the difference between 100 per cent and the totals of the bonds and preferred, or 70 per cent in our sample company. You will want to remember that the most valuable method of determining the common stock ratio is in combination with reserve and surplus. The surplus, as we have noted, is additional backing for the common stock and usually represents either original funds paid in to the company in excess of the stated value of the common stock (capital surplus), or undistributed earnings (earned surplus).

Most investment analysts carefully examine industrial companies that have more than about a quarter of their capitalization represented by bonds, while common stock should total at least as much as all senior securities (bonds and preferred issues). When this is not the case, companies often find it difficult to raise new capital. Banks don't like to lend them money because of the already large debt, and it is sometimes difficult to sell common stock because of all the bond interest or preferred dividends that must be paid before anything is available for the common stockholder.

Railroads and public utility companies are exceptions to most of the rules of thumb that we use in discussing The ABC Manufacturing Company, Inc. Their situation is different because of the tremendous amounts of money they have invested in their fixed assets., their small inventories and the ease with which they can collect their receivables. Senior securities of railroads and utility companies frequently amount to more than half of their capitalization. Speculators often interest themselves in companies that have a high proportion of debt or preferred stock because of the *leverage factor*. A simple illustration will show why. Let us take, for example, a company with $10,000,000 of 4 per cent bonds outstanding. If the company is earning $440,000 before bond interest, there will be only $40,000 left for the common stock ($10,000,000 at 4% equals $400,000). However, an increase of only 10 per cent in earnings (to $484,000) will leave $84,000 for common stock dividends, or an increase of more than 100 per cent. If there is only a small common issue, the increase in earnings per share would appear very impressive.

You have probably already noticed that a decline of 10 per cent in earnings would not only wipe out everything available for the common stock, but result in the company being unable to cover its full interest on its bonds without dipping into surplus. This is the great danger of so-called high leverage stocks and also illustrates the fundamental weakness of companies that have a disproportionate amount of debt or preferred stock. Investors would do well to steer clear of them. Speculators, however, will continue to be fascinated by the market opportunities they offer.

## THE INCOME ACCOUNT

The fundamental soundness of a company, as shown by its balance sheet, is important to investors, but of even greater interest is the record of its operation. Its financial structure shows much of its ability to weather storms and pick up speed when times are good. It is the income record, however, that shows us how a company is actually doing and gives us our best guide to the future.

The *Consolidated Income and Earned Surplus* account of our company is stated on the next page. Follow the items given there and we will find out just how our company earned its money, what it did with its earnings, and what it all means in terms of our three classes of securities. We have used a combined income and surplus account because that is the form most frequently followed by industrial companies. However, sometimes the two statements are given separately. Also, a variety of names are used to describe this same part of the financial report. Sometimes it is called profit and loss account, sometimes *record of earnings,* and, often, simply *income account.* They are all the same thing.

The details that you will find on different income statements also vary a great deal. Some companies show only eight or ten separate items, while others will give a page or more of closely spaced entries that break down each individual type of revenue or cost. We have tried to strike a balance between extremes; give the major items that are in most income statements, omitting details that are only interesting to the expert analyst.

The most important source of revenue always makes up the first item on the income statement. In our company, it is *Net Sales* (item "a"). If it were a railroad or a utility instead of a manufacturer, this item would be called *gross revenues.* In any case, it represents the money paid into the company by its customers. Net sales are given to show that the figure represents the amount of money actually received after allowing for discounts and returned goods.

Net sales or gross revenues, you will note, is given before any kind of miscellaneous revenue that might have been received from investments, the sale of company property, tax refunds, or the like. A well-prepared income statement is always set up this way so that the stockholder can estimate the success of the company in fulfilling its major job of selling goods or service. If this were not so, you could not tell whether the company was really losing or making money on its operations, particularly over the last few years when tax rebates and other unusual things have often had great influence on final net income figures.

## COST OF SALES

A general heading, *Cost of Sales, Expenses and Other Operating Charges* (item "b") is characteristic of a manufacturing company, but a utility company or railroad would call all of these things *operating expenses.*

The most important subdivision is *Cost of Goods Sold* (item "c"). Included under cost of goods sold are all of the expenses that go directly into the manufacture of the products the company sells -- raw materials, wages, freight, power, and rent. We have lumped these expenses together, as many companies do. Sometimes, however, you will find each item listed separately. Analyzing a detailed income account is a pretty technical operation and had best be left to the expert.

## The ABC Manufacturing Company, Inc.
### CONSOLIDATED INCOME AND EARNED SURPLUS
### For the Year Ended December 31

| Item | | | |
|---|---|---|---|
| a. | Sales | | $10,000,000 |
| b. | COST OF SALES, EXPENSES AND OTHER OPERATING CHARGES: | | |
| c. | Cost of Goods Sold | $7,000,000 | |
| d. | Selling, Administrative & Gen. Expenses | 500,000 | |
| e. | Depreciation | 200,000 | |
| f. | Maintenance and Repairs | 400,000 | |
| g. | Taxes (Other than Federal Inc. Taxes) | 300,000 | 8,400,000 |
| h. | NET PROFIT FROM OPERATIONS | | $ 1,600,000 |
| i. | OTHER INCOME: | | |
| j. | Royalties and Dividends | $ 250,000 | |
| k. | Interest | 25,000 | 275,000 |
| l. | TOTAL | | $ 1,875,000 |
| m. | INTEREST CHARGES: | | |
| n. | Interest on Funded Debt | $ 70,000 | |
| o. | Other Interest | 20,000 | 90,000 |
| p. | NET INCOME BEFORE PROVISION FOR FED. INCOME TAXES | | $ 1,785,000 |
| q. | PROVISION FOR FEDERAL INCOME TAXES | | 678,300 |
| r. | NET INCOME | | $ 1,106,700 |
| s. | DIVIDENDS: | | |
| t. | Preferred Stock - $5.00 Per Share | $ 50,000 | |
| u. | Common Stock - $1.00 Per Share | 400,000 | |
| v. | PROVISION FOR CONTINGENCIES | 200,000 | 650,000 |
| w. | BALANCE CARRIED TO EARNED SURPLUS | | $ 456,700 |
| x. | EARNED SURPLUS – JANUARY 1 | | 3,073,000 |
| y. | EARNED SURPLUS – DECEMBER 31 | | $ 3,530,000 |

We have shown separately, opposite "d," the *Selling, Administrative and General Expenses* of the past year. Unfortunately, there is little uniformity among companies in their treatment of these important non-manufacturing costs. Our figure includes the expenses of management; that is, executive salaries and clerical costs; commissions and salaries paid to salesmen; advertising expenses, and the like.

*Depreciation* ("e") shows us the amount that the company transferred from income during the year to the depreciation reserve that we ran across before as item "11" on the balance sheet (page 2). Depreciation must be charged against income unless the company is going to live on its own fat, something that no company can do for long and stay out of bankruptcy.

## MAINTENANCE

*Maintenance and Repairs* (item "f") represents the money spent to keep the plant in good operating order. For example, the truck that we mentioned under depreciation must be kept running day by day. The cost of new tires, recharging the battery, painting and mechanical repairs are all maintenance costs. Despite this day-to-day work on the truck, the company must still provide for the time when it wears out -- hence, the reserve for depreciation.

You can readily understand from your own experience the close connection between maintenance and depreciation. If you do not take good care of your own car, you will have to buy a new one sooner than you would had you maintained it well. Corporations face the same problem with all of their equipment. If they do not do a good job of maintenance, much more will have to be set aside for depreciation to replace the abused tools and property.

*Taxes* are always with us. A profitable company always pays at least two types of taxes. One group of taxes are paid without regard to profits, and include real estate taxes, excise taxes, social security, and the like (item "g"). As these payments are a direct part of the cost of doing business, they must be included before we can determine the *Net Profit From Operations* (item "h").

*Net Profit from Operations* (sometimes called *gross profit)* tells us what the company made from manufacturing and selling its products. It is an interesting figure to investors because it indicates .how efficiently and successfully the company operates in its primary purpose as a creator of wealth. As a glance at the income account will tell you, there are still several other items to be deducted before the stockholder can hope to get anything. You can also easily imagine that for many companies these other items may spell the difference between profit and loss. For these reasons, we use net profit from operations as an indicator of progress in manufacturing and merchandising efficiency, not as a judge of the investment quality of securities.

*Miscellaneous Income* not connected with the major purpose of the company is generally listed after net profit from operations. There are quite a number of ways that corporations increase their income, including interest and dividends on securities they own, fees for special services performed, royalties on patents they allow others to use, and tax refunds. Our income statement shows *Other Income* as item "i," under which is shown income from *Royalties and Dividends* (item "j"), and, as a separate entry, *Interest* (item "k") which the company received from its bond investments. The *Total* of other income (item t1t?) shows us how much The ABC Manufacturing Company received from so-called *outside activities.* Corporations with diversified interests often receive tremendous amounts of *other income.*

INTEREST CHARGES

There is one other class of expenses that must be deducted from our income before we can determine the base on which taxes are paid, and that is *Interest Charges* (item "m"). As our company has $2,000,000 worth of 3 1/2 per cent bonds outstanding, it will pay *Interest on Funded Debt* of $70,000 (item "n"). During the year, the company also borrowed money from the bank, on which it, of course, paid interest, shown as *Other Interest* (item "o").

*Net Income Before Provision for Federal Income Taxes* (item "p") is an interesting figure for historical comparison. It shows us how profitable the company was in all of its various operations. A comparison of this entry over a period of years will enable you to see how well the company had been doing as a business institution before the Government stepped in for its share of net earnings. Federal taxes have varied so much in recent years that earnings before taxes are often a real help in judging business progress.

A few paragraphs back we mentioned that a profitable corporation pays two general types of taxes. We have already discussed those that are paid without reference to profits. *Provision for Federal Income Taxes* (item "q") is ordinarily figured on the total income of the company after normal business expenses, and so appears on our income account below these charges. Bond interest, for example, as it is payment on a loan, is deducted beforehand. Preferred and common stock dividends, which are *profits* that go to owners of the company, come after all charges and taxes.

## NET INCOME

After we have deducted all of our expenses and income taxes from total income, we get *Net Income* (item "r"). Net income is the most interesting figure of all to the investor. Net income is the amount available to pay dividends on the preferred and common stock. From the balance sheet, we have learned a good deal about the company's stability and soundness of structure; from net profit from operations, we judge whether the company is improving in industrial efficiency. Net income tells us whether the securities of the company are likely to be a profitable investment.

The figure given for a single year is not nearly all of the story, however. As we have noted before, the historical record is usually more important than the figure for any given year. This is just as true of net income as any other item. So many things change from year to year that care must be taken not to draw hasty conclusions. During the war, Excess Profits Taxes had a tremendous effect on the earnings of many companies. In the next few years, *carryback tax credits* allowed some companies to show a net profit despite the fact that they had operated at a loss. Even net income can be a misleading figure unless one examines it carefully. A rough and easy way of judging how *sound* a figure it is would be to compare it with previous years.

The investor in stocks has a vital interest in *Dividends* (item "s"). The first dividend that our company must pay is that on its *Preferred Stock* (item "t"). Some companies will even pay preferred dividends out of earned surplus accumulated in the past if the net income is not large enough, but such a company is skating on thin ice unless the situation is most unusual.

The directors of our company decided to pay dividends totaling $400,000 on the *Common Stock,* or $1 a share (item "u"). As we have noted before, the amount of dividends paid is not determined by net income, but by a decision of the stockholders' representatives - the company's directors. Common dividends, just like preferred dividends, can be paid out of surplus if there is little or no net income. Sometimes companies do this if they have a long history of regular payments and don't want to spoil the record because of some special temporary situation that caused them to lose money. This occurs even less frequently and is more *dangerous* than paying preferred dividends out of surplus.

It is much more common, on the contrary, to *plough earnings back into the business* -- a phrase you frequently see on the financial pages and in company reports. The directors of our typical company have decided to pay only $1 on the common stock, though net income would have permitted them to pay much more. They decided that the company should *save* the difference.

The next entry on our income account, *Provision for Contingencies* (item "v"), shows us where our reserve for contingencies arose. The treasurer of our typical company has put the provision for contingencies after dividends. However, you will discover, if you look at very many financial reports, that it is sometimes placed above net income.

All of the net income that was not paid out as dividends, or set aside for contingencies, is shown as *Balance Carried to Earned Surplus* (item "w"). In other words, it is kept in the business. In previous years, the company had also earned more than it paid out so it had already accumulated by the beginning of the year an earned surplus of $3,073,000 (item "x"). When we total the earned surplus accumulated during the year to that which the company had at the first of the year, we get the total earned surplus at the end' of the year (item "y"). You will notice that the total here is the same as that which we ran across on the balance sheet as item 27.

Not all companies combine their income and surplus account. When they do not, you will find that *balance carried to surplus will* be the last item on the income account. The statement of consolidated surplus would appear as a third section of the corporation's financial report. A separate surplus account might be used if the company shifted funds for reserves to surplus during the year or made any other major changes in its method of treating the surplus account.

## ANALYZING THE INCOME ACCOUNT

The income account, like the balance sheet, will tell us a lot more if we make a few detailed comparisons. The size of the totals on an income account doesn't mean much by itself. A company can have hundreds of millions of dollars in net sales and be a very bad investment. On the other hand, even a very modest profit in round figures may make a security attractive if there are only a small number of shares outstanding.

Before you select a company for investment, you will want to know something of its *margin of profit,* and how this figure has changed over the years. Finding the margin of profit is very simple. We just divide the net profit from operations (item "h") by net sales (item "a"). The figure we get (0.16) shows us that the company make a profit of 16 per cent from operations. By itself, though, this is not very helpful. We can make it significant in two ways.

In the first place, we can compare it with the margin of profit in previous years, and, from this comparison, learn if the company excels other companies that do a similar type of business. If the margin of profit of our company is very low in comparison with other companies in the same field, it is an unhealthy sign. Naturally, if it is high, we have grounds to be optimistic.

Analysts also frequently use *operating ratio* for the same purpose. The operating ratio is the complement of the margin of profit. The margin of profit of our typical company is 16. The operating ratio is 84. You can find the operating ratio either by subtracting the margin of profit from 100 or dividing the total of operating costs ($8,400,000) by net sales ($10,000,000).

The margin of profit figure and the operating ratio, like all of those ratios we examined in connection with the balance sheet, give us general information about the company, help us judge its prospects for the future. All of these comparisons have significance for the long term as they tell us about the fundamental economic condition of the company. But you still have the right to ask: *"Are the securities good investments for me now?"*

Investors, as opposed to speculators, are primarily interested in two things. The first is safety for their capital and the second, regularity of income. They are also interested in the rate of return on their investment but, as you will see, the rate of return will be affected by the importance placed on safety and regularity. High income implies risk. Safety must be bought by accepting a lower return.

The safety of any security is determined primarily by the earnings of the company that are available to pay interest or dividends on the particular issue. Again, though, round dollar figures aren't of much help to us. What we want to know is the relationship between the total money available and the requirements for each of the securities issued by the company.

## INTEREST COVERAGE

As the bonds of our company represent part of its debt, the first thing we want to know is how easily the company can pay the interest. From the income account we see that the company had total income of $1,875,000 (item "1"). The interest charge on our bonds each year is $70,000 (3 1/2 per cent of $2,000,000 - item 21 on the balance sheet). Dividing total income by bond interest charges ($1,875,000 by $70,000) shows us that the company earned its bond interest 26 times over. Even after income taxes, bond interest was earned 17 times, a method of testing employed by conservative analysts. Before an industrial bond should be considered a safe investment, most analysts say that the company should earn interest charges several times over, so our company has a wide margin of safety.

To calculate the *preferred dividend coverage* (i.e., the number of times preferred dividends were earned), we must use net income as our base, as Federal Income Taxes and all interest charges must be paid before anything is available for stockholders. As we have 10,000 shares of $100 par value of preferred stock which pays a dividend of 5 per cent, the total dividend requirement for the preferred stock is $50,000 (items 24 on the balance sheet and "t" on the income account).

## EARNINGS PER COMMON SHARE

The buyer of common stocks is often more concerned with the earnings per share of his stock than he is with the dividend. It is usually earnings per share or, rather, prospective earnings per share, that influence stock market prices. Our income account does not show the earnings available for the common stock, so we must calculate it ourselves. It is net income less preferred dividends (items "r" - "t"), or $1,056,700. From the balance sheet, we know that there are 400,000 shares outstanding, so the company earned about $2.64 per share.

All of these ratios have been calculated for a single year. It cannot be emphasized too strongly, however, that the *record* is more important to the investor than the report of any single year. By all the tests we have employed, both the bonds and the preferred stock of our typical company appear to be very good investments,, if their market prices were not too high. The investor would want to look back, however, to determine whether the operations were reasonably typical of the company.

Bonds and preferred stocks that are very safe usually sell at pretty high prices, so the yield to the investor is small. For example, if our company has been showing about the same coverage on its preferred dividends for many years and there is good reason to believe that the future will be equally kind, the company would probably replace the old 5 per cent preferred with a new issue paying a lower rate, perhaps 4 per cent.

## STOCK PRICES

As the common stock does not receive a guaranteed dividend, its market value is determined by a great variety of influences in addition to the present yield of the stock measured by its dividends. The stock market, by bringing together buyers and sellers from all over the world, reflects their composite judgment of the present and future value of the stock. We cannot attempt here to write a treatise on the stock market. There is one important ratio, however, that every common stock buyer considers. That is the ratio of earnings to market price.

The so-called *price-earnings ratio is* simply the earnings per share on the common stock divided into the market price. Our typical company earned $2.64 a common share in the year, If the stock were selling at $30 a share, its price-earnings ratio would be about 11.4. This is the basic figure that you would want to use in comparing the common stock of this particular company with other similar stocks.

# IMPORTANT TERMS AND CONCEPTS

LIABILITIES
: WHAT THE COMPANY OWES -- + RESERVES + SURPLUS + STOCKHOLDERS INTEREST IN THE COMPANY

ASSETS
: WHAT THE COMPANY OWNS -- + WHAT IS OWED TO THE COMPANY

FIXED ASSETS
: MACHINERY, EQUIPMENT, BUILDINGS, ETC.

EXAMPLES OF FIXED ASSETS
: DESKS, TABLES, FILING CABINETS, BUILDINGS, LAND, TIMBERLAND, CARS AND TRUCKS, LOCOMOTIVES AND FREIGHT CARS, SHIPYARDS, OIL LANDS, ORE DEPOSITS, FOUNDRIES

EXAMPLES OF:

PREPAID EXPENSES
: PREPAID INSURANCE, PREPAID RENT, PREPAID ROYALTIES AND PREPAID INTEREST

DEFERRED CHARGES
: AMORTIZATION OF BOND DISCOUNT, ORGANIZATION EXPENSE, MOVING EXPENSES, DEVELOPMENT EXPENSES

ACCOUNTS PAYABLE
: BILLS THE COMPANY OWES TO OTHERS

BONDHOLDERS ARE CREDITORS
: BOND CERTIFICATES ARE IOU'S ISSUED BY A COMPANY BACKED BY A PLEDGE

BONDHOLDERS ARE OWNERS
: A STOCK CERTIFICATE IS EVIDENCE OF THE SHAREHOLDER'S OWNERSHIP

EARNED SURPLUS
: INCOME PLOWED BACK INTO THE BUSINESS

NET SALES
: GROSS SALES MINUS DISCOUNTS AND RETURNED GOODS

NET INCOME
: = TOTAL INCOME MINUS ALL EXPENSES AND INCOME TAXES

# ANSWER SHEET

TEST NO. _____ PART _____ TITLE OF POSITION _____

(AS GIVEN IN EXAMINATION ANNOUNCEMENT - INCLUDE OPTION, IF ANY)

PLACE OF EXAMINATION _____

(CITY OR TOWN)      (STATE)      DATE _____

RATING

## USE THE SPECIAL PENCIL. MAKE GLOSSY BLACK MARKS.

Make only ONE mark for each answer. Additional and stray marks may be counted as mistakes. In making corrections, erase errors COMPLETELY.

# ANSWER SHEET

TEST NO. ____________ PART ______ TITLE OF POSITION ______________________________
(AS GIVEN IN EXAMINATION ANNOUNCEMENT - INCLUDE OPTION, IF ANY)

PLACE OF EXAMINATION ______________________ (CITY OR TOWN) ______________ (STATE) DATE ________

| RATING |
|---|
| |

USE THE SPECIAL PENCIL. MAKE GLOSSY BLACK MARKS.

| | | | | |
|---|---|---|---|---|
| 1 A B C D E | 26 A B C D E | 51 A B C D E | 76 A B C D E | 101 A B C D E |
| 2 A B C D E | 27 A B C D E | 52 A B C D E | 77 A B C D E | 102 A B C D E |
| 3 A B C D E | 28 A B C D E | 53 A B C D E | 78 A B C D E | 103 A B C D E |
| 4 A B C D E | 29 A B C D E | 54 A B C D E | 79 A B C D E | 104 A B C D E |
| 5 A B C D E | 30 A B C D E | 55 A B C D E | 80 A B C D E | 105 A B C D E |
| 6 A B C D E | 31 A B C D E | 56 A B C D E | 81 A B C D E | 106 A B C D E |
| 7 A B C D E | 32 A B C D E | 57 A B C D E | 82 A B C D E | 107 A B C D E |
| 8 A B C D E | 33 A B C D E | 58 A B C D E | 83 A B C D E | 108 A B C D E |
| 9 A B C D E | 34 A B C D E | 59 A B C D E | 84 A B C D E | 109 A B C D E |
| 10 A B C D E | 35 A B C D E | 60 A B C D E | 85 A B C D E | 110 A B C D E |

Make only ONE mark for each answer. Additional and stray marks may be counted as mistakes. In making corrections, erase errors COMPLETELY.

| | | | | |
|---|---|---|---|---|
| 11 A B C D E | 36 A B C D E | 61 A B C D E | 86 A B C D E | 111 A B C D E |
| 12 A B C D E | 37 A B C D E | 62 A B C D E | 87 A B C D E | 112 A B C D E |
| 13 A B C D E | 38 A B C D E | 63 A B C D E | 88 A B C D E | 113 A B C D E |
| 14 A B C D E | 39 A B C D E | 64 A B C D E | 89 A B C D E | 114 A B C D E |
| 15 A B C D E | 40 A B C D E | 65 A B C D E | 90 A B C D E | 115 A B C D E |
| 16 A B C D E | 41 A B C D E | 66 A B C D E | 91 A B C D E | 116 A B C D E |
| 17 A B C D E | 42 A B C D E | 67 A B C D E | 92 A B C D E | 117 A B C D E |
| 18 A B C D E | 43 A B C D E | 68 A B C D E | 93 A B C D E | 118 A B C D E |
| 19 A B C D E | 44 A B C D E | 69 A B C D E | 94 A B C D E | 119 A B C D E |
| 20 A B C D E | 45 A B C D E | 70 A B C D E | 95 A B C D E | 120 A B C D E |
| 21 A B C D E | 46 A B C D E | 71 A B C D E | 96 A B C D E | 121 A B C D E |
| 22 A B C D E | 47 A B C D E | 72 A B C D E | 97 A B C D E | 122 A B C D E |
| 23 A B C D E | 48 A B C D E | 73 A B C D E | 98 A B C D E | 123 A B C D E |
| 24 A B C D E | 49 A B C D E | 74 A B C D E | 99 A B C D E | 124 A B C D E |
| 25 A B C D E | 50 A B C D E | 75 A B C D E | 100 A B C D E | 125 A B C D E |